'Spiritual formation lies at the heart of the Christian worldview, yet often becomes the caboose instead of the engine. In this book, Kate provides a thoughtful framework for understanding the pull of the Spirit towards a spirituality that arises from Scripture, life testing and purposeful development.'
Ted Esler PhD, President, Missio Nexus

'This book literally sings with the life of someone who delights in and loves Jesus, and continues to be formed in his image. It is not so much an academic writing on spiritual disciplines to deepen your life in Christ; rather, it is a long poem witnessing Kate's life formed in Christ, and the very clear and helpful ways this formation takes place. Reading the pages of her lived experiences, linked with the sacred Scriptures and searing questions, I am prodded and prompted to deepen my own life in Christ, and to mirror the purity with which she enjoys the blessed Trinity's presence. What a gift to read such a deeply personal, yet wholly applicable, template for our enduring formation in Jesus and the inevitable call to mission that follows such a depth of personal abandonment in him.'
Revd Dr Gayle Hill, former Mission Catalyst Leader, Baptist Union of Victoria, and Interim Pastor, West Melbourne Baptist Church

'*Shaped by the Spirit* is a fresh wind blowing into a familiar topic. Forming people into the image of Christ is at the core of the mission of God, and Kate diligently mines Scripture and literature to bring a unique perspective. I was personally challenged and encouraged as I read and reflected. Her questions at the end of each chapter alone are worth the book's price, but there is much more value in these pages. I highly recommend this book for personal formation as well as for those who are seeking to develop others.'
T. J. MacLeslie, author of *Designed for Relationship*

'In an age of great uncertainty and increasingly manic attempts to keep pace, *Shaped by the Spirit* speaks to us in the midst of the storm with that powerful "gentle whisper" (1 Kings 19:12 NLT). The beautifully crafted prose invites us to pause and consider the multifaceted ways we are formed, ultimately for God's purposes.

'This is a well-grounded book on spiritual formation, good for individual reflection but even better for helping groups of people understand one another at a much deeper level. With it we can dive into our inner worlds, discover a Spirit-filled image of God there, and take that forth with ever-increasing Christlikeness into the wider world, confident in our collective vision for blessing the nations.'
Dr Jay Mātenga, Executive Director, WEA Mission Commission

'Kate brings a fresh vision of spiritual formation. She weaves together biblical teaching with significant contributions from a broad group of thoughtful scholars and practitioners. Then she consistently illustrates the insights with her own global experiences and those of Jesus' followers worldwide. Kate models the art of listening to people with sincere respect. Discerning the work of the Spirit through those conversations, she shares the insights to expand our understanding of the nature of being formed. Kate has given us a great resource to help us as outward-focused people.'
Douglas McConnell PhD, Provost Emeritus and Senior Professor of Leadership and Intercultural Studies, Fuller Theological Seminary

'Kate invites us to pause and ponder, examining how God shapes us – not as a navel-gazing exercise, but one that helps us to be outward-focused as we share God's love with others. Her intertwining of various strands weaves together a Spirit-breathed creation that will challenge and inspire. I pray the Spirit uses her words as he shapes and forms you.'
Amy Boucher Pye, Spiritual Director and author of *Transforming Love*

'The Spirit's work in shaping us into Christlikeness is often perceived as hidden and mysterious. In this compelling and practical book, Kate opens our eyes to see his transformative power so vividly in our distinct life narratives. She vulnerably shares stories and theological insights, and asks thought-provoking questions throughout. I am challenged by the prayerful posture necessary to yield to the Spirit's work in our continual forming and filling, and for the sake of pouring out again. A must-read for anyone desiring a greater awareness of the Spirit's work in shaping them for a purpose beyond themselves.'
Kaye Redman, artist and creative educator

'This is a beautifully written book! It is packed with much-needed, gentle wisdom for all of us who long to be more profoundly shaped by the Spirit. I found myself lingering over each page, feeling alternately encouraged and quietly convicted – at a time when I had been experiencing my own time of spiritual weariness. It was exactly what I needed, perhaps, in no small part, due to Kate's close walk with Jesus, her love of the word, and her missional heart. May the Lord use this book for all his wonderful, redemptive purposes in the world.'
Naomi Reed, speaker and author of *My Seventh Monsoon*, *Heading Home*, *Finding Faith* and *A Time to Hope*

'I happened to be visiting Florence during the time that I was reading *Shaped by the Spirit*. Walking down the Galleria dell'Accademia towards Michelangelo's statue of David, I saw the half-finished statues and was reminded of this profound metaphor that Kate had used to emphasise the need for us to be willing to allow the Holy Spirit to shape us into the image of Christ. We are born of the Spirit, but are incomplete; as Kate puts it, masterpieces in the making.

'As leaders engaging with ministers of the gospel who live and serve in some of the most challenging places in the world, one of our aims is to help our gospel workers grow in resilience. The reality is that we very quickly reach the end of our natural talent, reserves, wisdom and strength in ministry at one time or another. We need to know how to tap into the strength and resource that is born of the Spirit. Whether we serve at home or overseas, the journey towards a more empowered spiritual life requires us to experience what it is to walk in the Spirit, pray in the Spirit, be led by the Spirit, and be attentive to the voice of the Spirit.

'We are formed by the Spirit for God's mission in the world, and it is transformed people who become a transforming presence in the world. *Shaped by the Spirit* is a timely reminder of the importance of the Holy Spirit in our faith journey.'
Dr Mark Syn, International Director, Pioneers

'Please go ahead and read *Shaped by the Spirit* if you want your world to be redefined by the Spirit. Read it against your lived experience with the anticipation of gaining a new perspective on God's work in and through your life. Being a friend of Dr Kate Pocklington and serving as Senior Pastor in her home church, I can hear her life speaking aloud through the pages of this book with depth and a sense of God's presence. May you share in a more profound friendship and fellowship with God the Spirit through reading this book.'
Revd Jun Tan, Senior Pastor, Balwyn Baptist Church

'In the discipleship of my youth, we were told not to be *conformed* to this world (Romans 12). Yet no one talked about how we were to be *formed*.

'Many of us have not paid nearly enough attention to what has formed and shaped us. In this practical and personal account, Kate guides the reader through various dimensions of how we have been formed, and the ways the gentle grace of God's Spirit wants to form us anew, for the purposes of God. I recommend this thoughtful and inspiring volume to all those who desire to know the transforming work of God in their lives.'

Jude Tiersma Watson, InnerChange Los Angeles, Senior Associate Professor of Urban Mission at Fuller Theological Seminary

'I have enjoyed the rich privilege of learning from Kate Pocklington in the journey that has led to this book. Kate's doctoral research explored the spiritual lives of West African mission leaders, and we sat in awe at the deep prayerfulness of our African sisters and brothers in Christ. Kate has drunk deeply from the spiritual well of world Christianity, and has brought these lessons into her own formation and the formation of others. *Shaped by the Spirit* blesses us with all that she has learned. We are fruitful in mission only as we abide in the Lord Jesus.'

Revd Dr David Williams, Director of Training and Development at St Andrew's Hall, CMS Australia

'Kate Pocklington's new book, *Shaped by the Spirit*, is a much needed how-to guide to spiritual formation – not merely for personal growth, but so a person can be equipped on an ongoing basis to fulfil the Great Commission by becoming more Christlike. This book is creative, beautifully written and timely, for in dark days when the world is suffering from war, pestilence, disease and famine, and death is stalking so many lands, this book gives us hope and assurance that God's yes to life is louder than death's no. Highly recommended.'

Ben Witherington III, Amos Professor of New Testament for Doctoral Studies, Asbury Theological Seminary

Kate Pocklington facilitates leadership development and mission formation within the Pioneers Oceania region. She enjoys teaching, speaking and mentoring, but delights most in expressing herself through writing. She earned a double master's degree from Asbury Theological Seminary and a Doctorate of Intercultural Studies, with a focus on prayer, from Fuller Theological Seminary. She completed her undergraduate studies through the Melbourne School of Theology, where she does some adjunct lecturing. Kate lives in Melbourne, Australia.

SHAPED BY THE SPIRIT

Being formed into an
outward-focused people

Kate Pocklington

First published in Great Britain in 2024

Society for Promoting Christian Knowledge
The Record Hall, 16–16A Baldwin's Gardens
London EC1N 7RJ
www.spckpublishing.co.uk

British Library Cataloguing-in-Publication Data
A catalogue record for this book is available from the British Library

ISBN 978–0–281–09040–2
Ebook ISBN 978–0–281–09041–9

1 3 5 7 9 10 8 6 4 2

Typeset by Fakenham Prepress Solutions
First printed in Great Britain by Clays Limited
Subsequently digitally printed in Great Britain
eBook by Fakenham Prepress Solutions

Produced on paper from sustainable sources

For

those who have helped shape me,
especially Dad and Mum,
my theological and personal anchors

those who long to be shaped

Contents

Contents

Part 3
LIFELONG FORMATION:
STRENGTHENING OUR INNER BEING

A word before

A road winds from Te Anau to Milford Sound, lush with ferns and *Lord of the Rings* forests. Before reaching this fjord in New Zealand's South Island, there is a stopping place simply named 'The Chasm'. A stone-smoothing river, travelling fast, passes trees dangling moss. Springs gush with plenty, fronds uncurl, trees bend with history, mountains hide behind the mist. As I look back at my photographs, I see a large rock seemingly moulded into a gnarled hand, fingernail outlined on the digit's tip. The stone glistens with the water collecting in small, moss-rimmed bowls. The river rushes fast through the chasm, sending up a cool spray. Shapes created by age, by pressure, by the constant liquid chase.

Our world, frail and falling apart, is in desperate need of people who have been formed by the gentle pressure and chase of God the Spirit. People who, in turn, desire to share that Christ-reflection with others. Those who want to live contagiously, spreading the life, truth and hope of Jesus to those around them. People who are Jesus-centred and outward-focused.

If we look around, the thread of the world is unravelling, and has been for millennia.

Covid-19 has irreparably stained our reality; floods, fire and financial crises, disease and disillusionment and displacement, pandemics and plagues have had a deep impact on individuals, communities and nations. Our world is in desperate need of hope, salvation, and a perspective larger than its own, a perspective given through the Creator God, the Saving Son, the Awakening Spirit. This world of ours needs people of faith and courage who have been forged and remodelled in the Spirit's shaping furnace. People with depth, with purpose. The world needs gospel-grounded, other-focused people.

One of my favourite quotes is by Richard Foster. He writes:

> In our day heaven and earth are on tiptoe waiting for the emergence of a Spirit-led, Spirit-intoxicated, Spirit-empowered people. All of creation watches expectantly for the springing up of a disciplined, freely gathered, martyr people who know in this life the life and power of the Kingdom of God.[1]

Men and women around the globe are waiting for the transformational gospel story to redefine their world in the best of ways, offered by a transformed people. However, the emergence of such a Spirit-led people can only occur with dimension and fullness if these same people are first Spirit-formed, fashioned by the powerful and yet gentle Spirit-breath, like a coastal shoreline, its sandstone cliffs shaped by the elements, formed and reformed over time.

That is what sparked me to write these pages, because formation in the deep places of our hearts and minds is foundational. Not surface formation, not therapeutic formation, not formation that we create or control, but formation that is yielded to the work of the Spirit in our lives, that moulds us to look more and more like Jesus, no matter what the cost, and that expresses itself in world witness. After all, being formed as gospel-orientated, outward-focused people is a Spirit-shaping process that brings change to every aspect of who we are – not allowing us to be satisfied with a change of thinking, but demanding a change of heart posture, leading to steps of obedience as we steward Jesus' vision and mission in the world. For, as Foster challenges us to see, heaven and earth are waiting with bated breath for a wholehearted people who, with arms flung wide open, say: 'Rework me into Christ-form so that Jesus is wanted and worshipped by more people and more peoples.'

This book is for those who desire to grow into clearer 'little Christs' and who, as they are moulded more into his reflection, are turned outwards, like a dancer pivoting by degrees. It is for people who desire to live persuasive lives, pointing others to Jesus. It is for communities of people who are given to others, who are serious about carrying on what Jesus started all those centuries ago. It is for people who invite the Spirit to invade their lives so that he can enable them to do this in the best way possible.

***

I wrote these pages during a three-month sabbatical. It was a time filled with ocean themes and tidal imagery, and God's joyous presence through his creation. Time and again the Lord provided what I came to call 'unexpected grace-gifts'.

To start this season, I accepted a surprising invitation to join some friends on a trip they were taking. It became a time of holy play, filled with the wonder of God's vividly beautiful creation and the easy response of worship.

On our return from this unexpected grace-gift, my home city went into its fourth Covid lockdown. So, rather than returning home, I stayed away. More unexpected grace-gifts, including a place to stay for two weeks, just metres from a seaside esplanade. Later, on my return home, when I asked God what was next, he dropped an idea into my mind which led to a house-sitting opportunity just minutes away from another sea view.

The tidal ebb and flow became a theme for this season, with the high tide of these unexpected grace-gifts filling me, the Father reminding me of his pleasure and love, his joy and goodness, of my place with him. The low tide, then, represented spilling out to others from this place of filling.

High tide, low tide.

Filling up and spilling out.

Wonder and worship.

But this sabbatical break was not wholly filled with wonder. One day I sat down to write, only to learn of the loss of a dear friend I have known for decades: a warm, funny, quirky man, unexpectedly gone. It left one of my friendship groups reeling, blanketed in sadness and feeling undone. On that day and during the weeks that followed, I found myself squeezing the Father's hand, knuckles white, sorrow thick. Filled up, this time with grief. Left wondering, instead of overtaken by wonder. One of our community amputated, and we felt the craving itch of the ghost limb. His life gifted for a time, but no more.

And yet another lengthy lockdown. Covid fatigue set in with earnest.

It took longer to be flooded by high tide, and I was slower to turn to worship. This time resolve, rather than wondrous response, arose. 'Help me to pay attention, Lord,' I prayed, even as I grieved. 'Help me to retain this posture of acknowledging you as the Source, of finding joy in receiving from you.' And Father kindly leaned down, planting his kiss on my forehead, like a parental blessing at a child's bedtime, reminding me of his response to Moses in Exodus 33:14,[2] and the promise of his presence.

We hold the tension of this rhythmic dance: high tide, low tide, gain, loss, wonder, worship . . . even as we wait. This is the place we inhabit, a place with a natural ebb and flow that forms and fashions, shapes and smooths, preparing us for his purposes.

This book is an offering from that sabbatical season, and from the many years of mission engagement leading up to it. It is for Jesus-following, other-orientated people. It is to remind us of our Father's deep love for us, and the Spirit's focused and joyful commitment to forming us more and more each day into the likeness of Christ – who is the central hope of world history and of our own stories. It is a reminder that the Spirit can take every aspect of our lives, breathe his reshaping life into it, and transform it into something that will honour God's name as we live and speak the compelling story of Jesus out to others.

In the pages to come, we will explore what it means to be shaped by the Spirit for God's purposes. In Part 1 we will reflect on the ideas of being formed *by* God the Spirit, *through* the pathway of prayer, and *for* God's mission in the world. In Part 2 we will go deeper into how we are formed for God's outward-focused purposes from a range of ingredients. That is, what we are formed *from*. Part 3 will investigate conduits of continuing formation.

This is not an academic book. Nor, ideally, is it a book to be rushed, but rather it is one where you can linger with the Spirit as he reveals or encourages or gently challenges you about certain themes raised. From Part 2 onwards, 'formation questions' are added at each chapter end. Use them as a guide. Some questions may resonate more than others. Some readers, though, may want to work their way through all six sequentially. Either way, I would invite you to reflect prayerfully on those questions, welcoming the Spirit as he continues his shaping of each one of us to more truly resemble Jesus as outward-focused people.

Father, we come to you partially formed.
Grateful for the work of the Son,
dependent on the committed shaping work of the Spirit.
Form us this day,
as we continue to spill you out to others
who do not yet know you.
Thank you in anticipation, Father, for your future work in us.

Part I

THE SHAPING PROCESS: BEING FORMED BY, THROUGH AND FOR

Unformed

There was a sense of anticipation as I turned the corner of the Galleria dell'Accademia in Florence, which holds Michelangelo's famous sculpture *David*. Walking into the hallway leading up to the spotlit statue, my eyes were immediately drawn to its grandeur. It was larger than life, with David's hands idly toying with the ends of the slingshot, his face pensive. It was only later that I noticed other sculptures.

In that same hallway leading up to the centre point of *David* sit four large blocks of marble. Of the full collection of six, known as the *Prisoners* or *Slaves*, two pieces are located in the Louvre, while the remaining four *Prisoners* act as a guard of honour to Michelangelo's *David*. They are fascinating. Trapped in various stages of completion, these undeveloped pieces possess a sense of movement, of emotion, of promise. An almost complete arm and torso, but an unformed back; a knee and front thigh smooth and ready to run, but without a calf or feet, imprisoned in stone and unable to break free. If you lean in closely, you can see the chisel marks, the tools that carefully cultivated shape, form, life. You can imagine Michelangelo's breath on the marble as he meticulously carved stone from here but left it there, drawing out a flesh-like roundness to the bodies, supple yet strong. Works of art. Masterpieces in the making. Unfinished, incomplete, waiting to be fully formed.

It reminds me of Ephesians 2:10 – how we, as God's people, are his handiwork, his works of art, his masterpieces, as various translations highlight. We too are unfinished, waiting as the renovation continues. Although the artist Michelangelo is long dead and unable to finish what he started, God, the supreme artist, is alive and actively at work in our lives. He has high commitment to the art projects that we represent, and he is exceptionally skilful with his chisel. I appreciate what Erwin Raphael McManus adds to this:

> For our lives to be works of art, we need to allow a lifetime of work. We must give God the time to make us works of art. We must press close to God and allow both the tenderness of his touch and pressure of his hands to shape us and mold us into someone we would not be without him. If we want our lives to be works of art, we must be willing to take the time and risk the intimacy required for creating an artisan life. We have to get close enough to allow the hands of God to press against us and reform us.[1]

In this shaping process, we are formed *by* the God of all things, with the Spirit as our active former. We are formed *through* conversation with him in prayer, this unique and intimate avenue of shaping. We are formed *for* his purposes, making a name, not for ourselves, but for God revealed in Jesus – seeing his glory and story, honour and renown spread out. After all, the best way to reach the world *for* Jesus is to look *like* Jesus. Our world witness 'is grounded in the kind of people we are being formed into. The quality of our presence is our mission.'[2] And we are formed *from* a myriad of materials that the Holy Artisan – God the Spirit – uses so creatively throughout the rolling years of our lives.

1

Formed by . . .

The Spirit as former

It is a mysterious image that we find in Genesis 1:2 – the 'Spirit of God . . . hovering over the surface of the waters',[1] bearing witness as the dark, empty and formless earth sparked into light and life. He breathed his shaping breath (*ruah* in Hebrew) to accompany the Father's words, summoning beauty and bounty out of the void. Sara Lubbers brings this scene to life:

> Just imagine! Darkness, thick and deep – rich with both the Author's presence and so much possibility. The Word hovered closely over this dark, watery canvas, so closely it could feel His warm breath as He spoke. Slowly, softly, He began to breathe words onto it; and as He did, a soft glow of light appeared . . .[2]

This Hebrew term *ruah*[3] – meaning breath, spirit, wind – is used a number of times (377) in a number of ways throughout the Old Testament. One of the significant ways it is applied is to create: giving birth to the stars (Psalm 33:6), creating life and renewing the face of the earth (Psalm 104:30). Again, we find it in Exodus 28:3 as the tabernacle, and all things related to it, takes form. Verses 1–8 of that chapter read as follows (the italics are mine):

> Call for your brother, Aaron, and his sons, Nadab, Abihu, Eleazar, and Ithamar. Set them apart from the rest of the people of Israel so they may minister to me and be my priests. Make sacred garments for Aaron that are glorious and beautiful.

Instruct all the skilled craftsmen whom I have filled with the *spirit of wisdom*. Have them make garments for Aaron that will distinguish him as a priest set apart for my service. These are the garments they are to make: a chestpiece, an ephod, a robe, a patterned tunic, a turban, and a sash. They are to make these sacred garments for your brother, Aaron, and his sons to wear when they serve me as priests. So give them fine linen cloth, gold thread, and blue, purple, and scarlet thread.

The craftsmen must make the ephod of finely woven linen and skillfully embroider it with gold and with blue, purple, and scarlet thread. It will consist of two pieces, front and back, joined at the shoulders with two shoulder-pieces. The decorative sash will be made of the same materials: finely woven linen embroidered with gold and with blue, purple, and scarlet thread.

The spirit of wisdom – the *ruah* of wisdom – filled these skilled artisans so that they could create garments that were 'glorious and beautiful' (v. 2). All the minute instructions are there in this passage. They fashioned and formed items out of fine linen and multicoloured threads, but for a purpose: to ensure that Aaron and his priests were set apart for their priestly roles. It does not stop there. Jump down to Exodus 31:1–11, especially the first few verses:

Then the LORD said to Moses, 'Look, I have specifically chosen Bezalel son of Uri, grandson of Hur, of the tribe of Judah. I have filled him with the Spirit of God, giving him great wisdom, ability, and expertise in all kinds of crafts. He is a master craftsman, expert in working with gold, silver, and bronze. He is skilled in engraving and mounting gemstones and in carving wood. He is a master at every craft!

'And I have personally appointed Oholiab son of Ahisamach, of the tribe of Dan, to be his assistant. Moreover, I have given

special skill to all the gifted craftsmen so they can make all the
things I have commanded you to make . . .'

Imagine being Bezalel. I wonder if he was already relatively
creative, or if the filling of the Spirit of God – the *ruah* of God –
supernaturally transformed him from someone who was obviously
lacking in creativity to someone who excelled? Either way, the text
makes it clear: the *ruah* brought an intelligence and expertise that
lifted him from being someone working with his hands to being a
master, not just of his own craft but of every craft. Others followed
suit to help fulfil the multiple commands with finesse and grace. In
Exodus 35:30–35 Bezalel's commission is echoed, but the English
Standard Version (esv) draws out a different nuance, indicating
that the filling of the Spirit of God enabled Bezalel 'to devise artistic
designs' (v. 32). The Spirit here is inspiring Bezalel not just to
complete the works but also to imagine and create a work of beauty.
The Spirit, the grand designer.

We see it again in the New Testament, this time using *pneuma*,
the Greek equivalent of *ruah* – again meaning breath, spirit, wind.
God continues his divine artistry, bringing together his power,
love and wisdom. We witness it supremely as Jesus was knitted
together in Mary's womb, formed by the Holy Spirit. Then, later, his
ministry was initiated by the 'Spirit of God descending like a dove
and settling on him' (Matthew 3:16). In the following chapter, led by
the Spirit, Jesus forged his purpose and set his sights and overcame
temptation. In Luke's Gospel we can recognise the Spirit's shaping
mark in Simeon's life, a man who lived in rhythm with the Spirit.
His encounter with the infant Jesus was prepared by the Spirit, like
an artist mixing paints and applying them to the canvas of this
divine moment (Luke 2:27–28).

The Gospel of John tells us again of the shaping breath of the
Spirit – that when he came to the original disciples, and comes
later to us, he came and comes to teach and remind us of all things

related to Jesus (John 14:26), continuing to reinvent his people in the image of Jesus so that we look more like him today than we did yesterday, more tomorrow than we do today, and so on. His tenacity is a powerful sign of love and fidelity. It is a love that sends us, gently turning us outwards and nudging us to step into God's mission in the world. For his *pneuma* breath readies us for being launched: Father to Son, Son to the disciples, and to us – an unfathomable comparison of grace (John 20:21–22).

We observe the Spirit configuring the Church in the Acts of the Apostles: instructing (1:2), baptising (1:5), granting courage and language and prophetic ability for witness (4:31; 2:4; 2:17–18), spotlighting sin and refining the Church of attempts at compartmentalisation (5:3), filling and setting aside people to serve as an answer to friction and division in the Church (6:2–3), drawing the boundaries of the sacred ground Stephen stepped into as the first martyr of the early church (7:55), painting the encounter between Philip and the Ethiopian eunuch (8:29), growing its numbers (9:31), forming Peter as a leader of the Church through encounters and leadings (10:19), beautifying the Church through greater diversity (10:45), expanding it through unique assignments and people (13:2, 4), mapping the believers' journey by both closing and opening doors at the appropriate time (16:6–8; 19:21), forming resilience (20:22–23) and creating roles (20:28), to name a good number of examples.

The *Pneuma* continued this work of shaping and reshaping, as Paul's writings portray. Romans 8 lingers on the mystery released when we surrender to the life-giving Spirit, inviting him to sculpt our thought-life, our wills, our desires, our emotions into Christ-form. Fear is cut out, and love is brought into fullness; old natures are removed, replaced by the new, marking God's holy exchange.

Paul uses another image in 2 Corinthians 3:3, depicting believers as a letter outlined and written in the Spirit's ink, signed by his imprint. However, it is 2 Corinthians 3:18 which clearly points out the Spirit's pleasure in the work of formation: 'And the Lord – who is the Spirit – makes us more and more like him as we are changed into his glorious image', with the maternal longing for full formation expressed in Galatians 4:19.[4] The Spirit is the one holding the pen, the sandpaper, the chisel. His purpose is to bring change, fashioning and forming, melding and moulding us to look and live like Jesus, the Christ, plain and simple.

It is a surrender that we often try to reclaim, once again seizing control of our lives. Not a good idea, Paul reminds us: 'After starting your new lives in the Spirit, why are you now trying to become perfect by your own human effort?' (Galatians 3:3). We forget just how much we need the Spirit to renew and reform our thoughts and attitudes so that our image reflects God (Ephesians 4:23–24). We need him to help us mirror his own character and nature to others, as the remainder of this Ephesians passage expresses, like a photographer's reflector, held at the right angle, bouncing a glow of light where shadows linger.

It is God the Spirit, bringing alive the work of God the Son, gifted by God the Father (Luke 24:49), who is the divine shaper. He is called the Spirit of Jesus (Acts 16:7), or the Spirit of Jesus Christ (Philippians 1:19); the Spirit of God, the Spirit of life or the life-giving Spirit (Romans 8); the Spirit of truth (John 14; 15; 16). God in action, executing his artistry within us.

But God is a gentleman. He does not force himself on us. Instead, he patiently waits for us to respond to his gentle pursuit, courting us, anticipating the day when we will give him full access to every corner of our lives. Harold Hoehner comments:

If believers were only filled with wisdom, the influence would be impersonal; however, the filling by the Spirit adds God's personal presence, influence, and enablement to walk wisely, all of which are beneficial to believers and pleasing to God. With the indwelling each Christian has all of the Spirit, but the command to be filled by the Spirit enables the Spirit to have all of the believer.[5]

Granting the Spirit – *ruah, pneuma* – full admission to our lives exponentially furthers the inner work of formation in us, allowing his breath free rein. After all, it is difficult for artists to work when the studio door is closed to them – easel and paints, trestle table and kiln lying on the other side of a barrier. When complete access is given, though, when we fling ourselves wide open in invitation to the Trinity – three in one, one in three – who encircles us in never-ending ministry, even when we do so with hesitation . . . this is when the masterpiece of our lives really takes definition under the genius of the Spirit.

2

Formed through . . .

Prayer – God's shaping pathway

Of all the pathways leading to formation for God's purposes, prayer is the most foundational. It involves listening to the Spirit, depending on the work of the Son and continually surrendering to the Father through personal conversation. It allows God's word and its earthy, everyday applications, intrinsic to our maturity, to be integrated into our lives. It is like a baker kneading dough, slowly working the ingredients into readiness. Without the stretching and folding movement of kneading, the leavening agents would not be released. Prayer 'is the central avenue the Holy Spirit uses to transform us'.[1] It is the baker's hands, so to speak, that stretch and fold us, generating transformation.

We can view prayer in a range of ways, but I have found that there are three elements that enliven it, leading to more meaningful formation. First, and perhaps obviously, prayer involves a relational conversation with God, natural and honest, which reflects a deepening trust in a caring God whom we know to be good, true and consistent. The relationship between God and Moses brings this to life, especially as it unfolded in the Tent of Meeting. There, 'the Lord would speak to Moses face to face, as one speaks to a friend' (Exodus 33:11). It is a strong and deeply personal image. In the New Testament, John's Gospel grants us a small glimpse of a tender moment, illustrating Jesus' simple trust of the Father as he thanks the Father for hearing him (John 11:41b–42).

Second, this communication is two-way. So often, our prayers are a one-way stream of words to God, but communicating with

God is not limited to the God-directed thanks and requests that often characterise our prayers. Or even perhaps to the well-known ACTS framework (Adoration, Confession, Thanksgiving and Supplication), truly helpful though it is at times. Prayer involves listening to and waiting on God. Luke's Gospel particularly emphasises prayer, with Jesus slipping off to spend time with the Father time and again, returning with a sense of resolve or clarity. In his sequel, the Acts of the Apostles, Luke gives us a handful of glimpses into Paul's experience of hearing from God: the Holy Spirit stopping Paul from entering Bithynia (Acts 16:7); Paul receiving a message from God in a vision of a Macedonian man calling for help (Acts 16:9); Paul hearing from God with words of reassurance (Acts 18:9–10). To paraphrase Bible teacher Jill Briscoe: 'Why is it that we ask things of God, but don't stay there long enough to hear a response?' Waiting to hear is an essential part of prayer.

Third, prayer involves a willingness to be changed and shaped, coupled with a posture of obedience, because '[o]bedience is faith in action. It is the outflow, the very test of love.'[2] One author writes, 'True prayer is habitually putting oneself under God's influence',[3] as we struggle to cede our will and way to God's will and way – with faith, hope and courage. Another writer notes that '[r]eal prayer is absolute self-surrender to, and absolute correspondence with, the mind, the will, the character, of God'.[4] Jesus' experience in Gethsemane brings this to life as he wrestles with and submits to the Father. Or consider Cornelius's response when God revealed himself through an angel (Acts 10:1–8). Cornelius heard (v. 5) and leapt into obedient, faith-filled action (v. 7). Peter, the second main character in this story, needed more convincing in the following passage, but he finally surrendered to God's plan in motion. Out of that place of relational, two-way communication with God, we hear, and are changed, bent to his will and turned outwards towards involvement in God's continuing pursuit of the world. As we yield to the Spirit's shaping through prayer, we are formed to partner with Christ in mysterious and wondrous ways, being invited deeper into his heart for the sake of the inhabitants of this aching earth.

Often, we view prayer as an arduous or boring obligation, rather than enjoying it as a warm welcome into the presence of the Trinity, a well-trodden and trusted path into God's heart. As one of my mentors said: 'The best thing that happened to me, after knowing Christ, was to discover the power of prayer.'

Back in 2015 I had the opportunity to learn about prayer and its profound role in forming the African arm of my organisational family as they engage in global mission. Tapping in to their deep reservoir of knowledge, experience and wisdom regarding prayer, I came away with a vivid cultural image of enjoying God's presence in prayer. 'In . . . African culture,' one gentleman explained, 'when we are cooking in our homes . . . we use firewood, and the longer you stay in the kitchen . . . [the more] you come back and smell of smoke.'[5] What a wonderful picture, reminding us to linger in the kitchen of God's presence so that, when we emerge, we smell of the smoke of his character and nature, his message and actions – a smoky fragrance rising to him, and inviting to others. One respected leader further emphasised how prayer nurtured this sense of intimacy and communion:

The relational aspect between myself and God developed as the prayer time increased . . . I discovered that prayer was two-way, not just me coming with a shopping list . . . and going away. I saw that if I spent time with Him, He spoke.[6]

The one brother whose words have lingered with me the longest, though, spoke from a place of deep, personal tragedy:

People thought . . . this guy will fold up . . . but . . . God has asked me to be here . . . I have known brothers in the ministry,

and they just throw in the towel. They just give up . . . because
. . . their relationship with God . . . their lives were not shaped
by their time with God.[7]

Their lives were not shaped by their time with God. The challenge
resounds, and yet it is not merely a challenge. It also touches on
a longing to be shaped, not by circumstance, but by God himself,
who works through and in circumstances. These words echo a grief
when such shaping does not happen, and a dependent relief when it
does. They reflect an awareness of lack, and a surrender to the one
who will take that want and fashion it with tenderness to display
more of himself. Another friend from this African community
brings this idea alive through these poignant words: 'I wouldn't
be here by now if I had not been somebody who was dedicated to
prayer, because, through prayer . . . God has taught me to surrender
to Him.'[8] Shaped by prayer, he was formed for God's outward-
focused purposes.

Such prayer nurtures a sense of dependence on and cooperation
with the Spirit. One brother spoke of his intention to 'find more
time in the presence of the Holy Spirit, trying to fellowship with
Him and listen. If He is a teacher, then I must be His student . . . it is
a transforming experience.'[9] This learning posture establishes us as
an apprentice to the Father, Son and Spirit of God, better learning
his ways and being entrusted with his mysteries. It is a model we see
echoed in the life of Jesus.

Jesus took on what N. T. Wright intriguingly identifies as an
apprentice model through his relationship with the Father, in
which, during his time on earth, he was learning from him.[10]
When there was a problem, or when the darkness of Gethsemane
arose, Jesus came to the Father, asking for advice, seeking the way
forward. This is a powerful concept as it highlights the level to which
Jesus relinquished himself to the Father in listening obedience. It
was particularly emphasised in the Father-and-Son relationship

expressed in John's Gospel, and Jesus' posture of remaining in the Father. The depth of communion and level of dependence which he modelled sets the tone for the personal, apprentice-type relationship that his disciples were invited into – as are we.

This kind of prayer – alive with the Spirit's pulse – is also costly. If we genuinely want to give the Spirit full access, if we genuinely long to look more like Jesus and live him out to others, then we need to mature our prayer life, having it as the warp and weft threads woven into the tapestry of our lives.

One woman brought this to life for me. Though young at the time, both she and her husband were deeply thoughtful, mature, committed followers of Jesus, intent on engaging in God's mission in the hard places of the world. Prayer marked both of their lives. I still remember her words:

> If something is a priority, we make time for it. We don't believe it's true until we act on it. I know what it costs to pray . . . all that can't be done in that time. But if I want prayer to shape our family, I need to steal that time away.
>
> With a little one who needs my constant attention, I only have her nap times as my 'free' time. There is always so much to do during those times. There will be a cost one way or another. But I want my relationship with the Lord to flavour my role as wife and mother. So, when I put her down for her first nap, that's when I spend time in [God's] word and in prayer. I choose it. I wouldn't trade it. But it costs me.

In our correspondence over the years, she continued to share about her journey of prayer. Admitting that prayer during nap times only works well with one child, or if multiple children have coinciding rest times, she expressed her constant need for focused and, if possible, uninterrupted time with the Lord, leading to a depth of abiding relationship. With both her and her husband recognising how this was equally integral for the two of them if their home was to be a Spirit-filled environment, her husband quickly began to prioritise her unbroken times with Jesus, making sacrifices to ensure this took place. This arrangement has continued, and it is a practical outworking of the couple's value of abiding in the Father. Later, she commented on her husband:

> He is very disciplined with his prayer. He has times where he spends intentional, focused time in prayer. And when he emerges from these times there is something different about his spirit, his nature. Like when Moses' face shone after being with God. This time he spends in prayer impacts the rest of his life as a husband. He wants to serve me more. He wants to be a better father.

It is not the time itself, costly though it is. It is the encounter that happens during this time that turns these minutes holy. It invites the Spirit to take the ember of a desire to live a Christ-formed life and fan it into flame so that it shapes family life, flavours being a wife and mother, and has an impact on being a husband, father, servant of others. Prayer does that. Rather, the Spirit does that through the pathway of prayer. Asking the question 'How can prayer shape my life?' is meaningful, but coupling it with a posture of consistent invitation to the Spirit to form us is vital for the ever-deepening process of becoming like Jesus.

We all have days when we are surprised by our responses, whether seen by others or not. We want to be a better father, like my friend's husband above, a better friend or leader or daughter or colleague or . . . (fill in the blank). Emotion may rise to the surface – flashes of anger, a sense that we have been wronged, frustration, envy, resentment, sadness. Taking those moments of the day and prayerfully sifting through them before the Lord deepens our perspective, moving the stormy whirling of our mind from ourselves to God. Prayer recalibrates our thoughts, reorientates our attitudes, realigns our wills. It takes fortitude and courage to look these ugly parts of ourselves in the eye, especially since they are often tucked out of sight until jolted to the surface and into view. I appreciate how Walter Wright affirms the helpful practice of prayerful, meditative reflection, as it is often through our awareness of vulnerability, weakness or sin that we dependently turn to the Father, continuing to retain the stance of an apprentice. He writes:

> I find that it is often during times of prayer that my mind sees the reality of my day from a different perspective. I keep paper and pencil with my Bible and allow myself to stop and write down ideas that come during prayer and reading. I am convinced that the meditative mind works differently from the reasoning mind. I see and think differently during . . . prayer and meditation.[11]

It is this kind of prayerful reflection that invites the Spirit of God – *ruah*, *pneuma* – to continue forming our character and nature. Then, when we are bumped and our inner responses burst or float to the surface, it is more likely that Jesus-esque qualities will emerge. The flavour of Christ is often observed more in *how* we do something than *what* we do. As we are formed to be outward-turned, gospel-orientated people, our character is shaped, our skills develop, our awareness is sharpened, our discernment is refined. All of these elements overlap. As we serve without thanks, we may realise that being noticed or affirmed by others is more important than we thought it was. As we learn the skill of another language, we may notice that we do not like being laughed at or seen as a child. As we develop our cultural intelligence in this multicultural world of ours, we may become aware of our sense of embedded entitlement, or be overwhelmed with grief at the sins of past generations that we represent. As we accept critique without encouragement, we may be reminded of where our identity has wandered off to and from whom it has wandered. As we are overwhelmed by the sadness, complexity or constant demands of a damaged world, we may admit our preference or need to be in control. Inviting the Spirit into these spaces, these emerging situations and contexts, and submitting ourselves to Christ as Jesus did to the Father is the evolving work of formation with an external application. We have been, are being, and will continue to be formed for God's mission in the world. The question is: how will we respond to the work of the Spirit through prayer?

3

Formed for . . .

Preparing a purpose

It would be tempting to view our transformation into the likeness of Christ as an end in itself. It may seem enough to wholeheartedly want and worship him. However, if we are genuinely seeking to mirror his heart and purpose, to be bent into his likeness, it means that we are being formed for something more, something greater. Our echo of Jesus is to reverberate like the long, sonorous tones of a gong, calling others to come meet him. Our lives are to ricochet sweetly like the voices of a French group I once heard, singing softly in a large vacant chamber of the ancient city of Petra, the acoustics causing their voices to swell and dive, drawing the curious to listen and enjoy. We are not simply to want and worship God revealed in Christ. We are to invite others to do so as well.

The prophet Isaiah says:

O LORD, you are our Father.
    We are the clay, and you are the potter.
    We all are formed by your hand.
(Isaiah 64:8)

This is true. Except a potter sits at a potting wheel with a purpose – to make cups or pots, vases or mugs. These items are to be filled, to be poured out. They – we – are vessels to be used for the Lord's glory, with his delight, in a joyous cycle of being filled and spilling out, filling up and spilling over. It is a compelling thought that we are being shaped to look more like Jesus so that we can represent him to others, drawing them to him, like the pull of a long cool drink on a scorching hot day.

In Ephesians 1:9–10 Paul hints at this – God's good plan, his mysterious will, is to bring everything under Christ. It is the attractional pull to the magnet of his glory and grace, his presence and power, his authority and awesomeness, his kingship, salvation, love and delight. He has chosen to use his people – his church (the grace-formed masterpieces of Ephesians 2:10) – as the conduits of this tug, along with the good things he has laid out for us to fulfil in his good time. We are shaped by the Spirit and formed with a purpose to bridge the divide between God revealed in Jesus and those who are yet to meet and know him deeply. We are formed *for* God's mission in the world.

The term 'formation' has its roots in the French word *former* (to form, mould, train, shape) and was initially used in the Roman Catholic Church when instructing novices, primarily regarding internal attitudes. Over the centuries it was applied to those training for the priesthood and was eventually adopted by the Anglican Church.

'Mission formation', or formation for God's mission in the world, is a close cousin to ministry formation or spiritual formation. The term is used widely by the Catholic Mission, with definitions that are compatible with Evangelical churches and mission organisations, although the outward expressions of these may differ. The Catholic Mission articulates mission formation as a transformational process, where the whole person is shaped – cognitive and spiritual aspects alike – 'to take up and carry on the mission of Jesus Christ in the world'.[1] What a wonderful phrase! *To take up and carry on the mission of Jesus Christ in the world* – a gentle ring of Jesus' call to his disciples to take up their cross and follow him. It is a summons to Christians to follow him daily, to follow him into the world around them, to follow him with cost and hope, to follow him in a way that bears witness. The Catholic Social Services Victoria (CSSV) expands this helpfully:

> When we talk of preparing people to share more effectively in the mission of Jesus, we speak of 'formation.' Formation is much more than training and education because it is about the internalisation of values, attitudes and ways of seeing, and the maturation of faith. It is something that we do in cooperation with God. Formation seeks to develop in us sensitivity to where God is leading our lives and our mission.[2]

It is something we do in cooperation with God, states the CSSV. Yes, particularly God the Spirit, whom the Father sent and Jesus anticipated with joy. We are transformed by him, but in collaboration with him. A range of practices are involved in this submissive relationship. It is a lifelong habit of mixing prayer and practice, study of and submission to God's word, meaningful reflection, robust conversations that may not always feel comfortable but expand our minds, and engaging with a variety of input that causes us to pause, percolate and pray some more before moving once again into practice. All of this so as to lead us to greater alignment with the heart of the Father, the mind of Christ, through the Spirit's gentle bending, as we, a Christ-centred, outward-focused people, interact with our reality. It is formation into the missional Christ, as there needs to be a correlation between formation and outward-focused, missional engagement. And it is continuously and eternally done for the sake of others, as Robert Mulholland writes in *Invitation to a Journey*.[3] Or, to draw our eyes even further afield, it is done for the sake of the nations, dispersed like dust in the wind across the world. Formation into God's mission, then, points to the transformational process of being shaped by the Spirit into the likeness of Christ, for the purpose of proclaiming and engaging in the mission of Christ here on earth in a way that spreads Jesus' holy fame.

The invitation into living outward-focused lives is for all of God's people who long to live a persuasive life-witness, pointing others to Jesus. Formation into witness-orientated people, more than anything, needs to include a posture that allows the Spirit to completely invade us. The Spirit influences our thinking (as highlighted in Romans 8:6), our values and behaviour (like the spiritual 'lego' built up in 2 Peter 1:5–8, with 'each dimension fitting into and developing the others'[4]), and the rhythms of our life (which marked the seven men, 'full of the Spirit and wisdom', chosen to assist the apostles in Acts 6:3). Mission formation is for outward-focused churches that are serious about having an impact on their communities for Christ. It is for other-focused communities that are intent on having an impact on those around them for Jesus. It is for diaspora disciples, those peoples dispersed and scattered across the globe; these brothers and sisters are often waiting for the invitation to contribute significantly to God's mission in the world, regardless of geographic location, wondering if their participation is truly valued. It is recognising and celebrating that we – each of us who follow Christ – have been and continue to be formed *by* God the Spirit; formed *through* relational prayer; formed *from* the stone blocks of our life experience; and formed *for* and *with* the purpose of living and speaking out God's kingdom as our combined focus and purpose in the world.

I think of my own small, multicultural church, filled with stories of God-at-work in the lives of those dispersed from their home nation and gathered in their new nation. It seems only a short time ago when Linda, always warm and welcoming, had her husband visiting from China, where he is based, running a business. The separation has been hard on them, while it also gave her the freedom to find and follow Jesus. Her husband was only in Australia for a few weeks, but Jesus was wooing him. At the end of one service, she dashed away from behind the movable stand where she was monitoring the video service for online participants, to whisper in our pastor's ear. He then turned to the rest of us and explained that Linda and her husband wanted to share something with the group. Her husband, speaking in Mandarin, shared his desire to follow Christ. Then. Right then. So our pastor led him in a simple prayer, and Linda's husband turned over control of his life to Jesus. Less than a week later, he was back in China. A new disciple birthed through the witness of his wife, the work of Christ and the draw of the Spirit. Missional living marked by a life in pursuit of the missional Christ.

'So the Word became human and made his home among us,' says John at the start of his Gospel (1:14). We, as human followers of Jesus, are both comfortable in the world and yet uneasy. We never fully fit in because of the greater home we anticipate. Yet we can wait patiently because this non-home base is made homelike by the Trinity taking up residence in the apartment block of our life (to paraphrase John 14:23), renovating it over time. Jesus, sent by the Father, came, emptying himself of the culture of heaven, taking on the culture of earth, and moved in. We, emptying ourselves of the lust and longings of earth, take on the cry and desire of heaven. 'In expectation of Christ, we . . . prepare ourselves to participate wholeheartedly in God's next move.'[5] We relocate and settle in, spread out, set up shop, go to work, move countries, join a book or rowing club. Like an Olympian wearing their uniform in a city street, we represent Jesus wherever we go. Our witness will be less obvious – not the loud green and yellow of an Aussie Olympian, perhaps – but, like an Olympian, it will seep into all parts of life. It will have an impact on our conversations and practices, how we spend time each day, our goals and hopes and dreams, our focus and finances and purpose. It will define our lives; or, more to the point, the one we are recommending will define us as he continues to form us to carry on his mission here on earth.

In this next part of the book, we will explore further what God (like Michelangelo with his blocks of marble) uses to fashion and form us *from* as we join him in his mission and purpose in the world. Each chapter will examine different materials – ten out of a plethora of choices – that the Spirit can use for his artwork as he shapes us into the likeness of Christ for the sake of those who have yet to meet, know, follow, worship and enjoy him.

Part 2

FORMED FROM: MATERIALS GOD USES TO SHAPE US FOR HIS MISSION IN THE WORLD

Recycled materials

A while ago I ordered some floating shelves for my kitchen. I found a guy on the internet who had made a hobby into a small business. He takes old, gnarled planks of timber, marked with stories of a past life, and reclaims them. With circular saw and smoothing planes, measures and squares, chisel and level, sandpaper, stain and oil, he takes the old and reshapes it, imagining something other, something new. I love those shelves. Every time I place something on them or take something from them, they bring me joy. Beauty from the old, the ugly, the no longer useful. Recycled, reformed, transformed.

God has an exceptional way of doing the same thing with us. He takes something – someone – and recycles it for his own purposes. We may be battered or fractured, proud or overly confident, hiding behind a mask or limping along. Perhaps we are drowning in blind spots or unaware of our own weaknesses, in a good place or a sad place. He takes each of us – with our own stories, influences and shaped by our own histories – and, if we let him, he reforms us.

We can think about it from a slightly different angle. God is the source of all things. All things are from him and through him and to him (Romans 11:36). By his grace, he has placed certain things in our hands, entrusting them to us. We hold these things, stewarding them well, passing them on to others. Part of what we pass on is the internal work of God the Spirit, shaping us into his likeness more and more each day, for the sake of others, for the sake of the nations; sharing his story and glory through the very way that he has fashioned us to look like him – and continues to do so. We each have something unique to pass on to others, a mutual exchange of sorts, giving and receiving as we move through life. Not because of our giftedness or role or status or charisma, but because of God's entrustment to us.

It is important to recognise the various materials the Spirit uses to create his masterpieces, deepening our communal awareness that we all have something to offer as the Father invites us to partner with Jesus, his Son (1 Corinthians 1:9), whether we are young believers new to the journey or weathered disciples with a string of accumulated years. Our contributions will look different, of course, but one is not more precious than another in the eyes of the one receiving these acts of life-worship or witness. The God-is-at-work-in-the-world life is an offering to God, living out the gift of his great story to others, enveloped in the wrapping paper of our own lives. Each roll of paper has its unique pattern, colour and texture, like the vibrant handmade paper draped in lines along an Indian market stall, each with its own weight and stamp. Every one of us within this collection of God's people brings something valuable to offer because of the One who has formed us, regardless of culture or gender, giftedness or confidence level.

There may be some readers who see their contribution as looking much more like paper strewn on the ground after being torn off a gift, rather than wrapping carefully folded around a present sitting invitingly under a Christmas tree, I say: take heart! There are people who need to hear about Jesus from those with creases and torn edges. I suspect that they would feel much more comfortable and hear more clearly from those such as yourself. Your life-experience grants you a dimension often absent in others. That is a part of the gift that you give, a fragile hue to your contribution, applied with the most delicate of longline paintbrushes.

4

Formed from . . . family

The role of family narrative in shaping us

The folder lies open before me. The blue ink is fading, as it does with old carbon copies. The typed letters are single spaced, crammed together to make the most of each page. The words are my grandfather's typed journal, written from April 1931 into the early months of 1938, although the latter years are remembered through spidery script in tiny notebooks.

In the pages collected, he tracks his lived missional experience along the borders of Tibet, his gradual language learning, and the people he met. He includes his travels to towns and villages in this mountainous region, covering over 25,000 *li* (6,000 miles) during his years there, his team strategy tied to giving out gospel literature. He tells of sickness and highs and lows; of his studies in the philosophy of Confucius and Mencius to give him deeper understanding of his new context; of his gratitude for his typewriter. He speaks of his fellow mission workers with respect and love, and of their practice of days of prayer and fasting, and his appreciation of these days. As the years passed into late 1936 and early 1937, he wrote about discipleship amid opium and idols, about broader travel, Tibetan church leaders, and his love of the local church. Finally, he began to describe the arthritis that crippled his left foot and would eventually take him from the land and people he had come to love.

Tucked into this collection of journals is an envelope containing folded sheets of yellow paper – an article called 'Tibet: The roof of the world'. Typing it for his mission organisation, Granddad brought alive some of his further travels into the Tibetan region. He writes:

> A few miles from one of the centres in which I worked there is a very pretty sacred mountain, which is the object of pilgrimages from all parts of Tibet . . . One day I met a man circumambulating the sacred mountain by making length-by-length prostrations along the road. It would take him about five months to cover the three hundred miles necessary to circle the mountain. The road was dusty and rough, stony and steep, and led over a cold mountain pass covered deep in snow. This was certainly the most extraordinary of all attempts to gain merit by works that I have witnessed . . . In the same way we find many prepared to go all lengths in duty and in pious, philanthropic works for salvation, whilst comparatively few accept the God appointed way through faith in the Saviour of the World.
>
> I offered this pilgrim my gospel portions. At first, he politely refused, explaining that he would crush them during his prostrations if he put them in the folds of his gown, the place where every Tibetan carries most of his gear, that is – his food bowl, snuff horn, money bag, prayer wheel, tobacco pouch, spare green-hide ropes, etc. After making three more prostrations the pilgrim surprised me by returning and asking for the books. He then placed them in behind his armpits, and thus, as he continued his meritorious pilgrimage, he carried with him two copies of the Word of God, which I prayed would tell him of the free unmerited grace of the Lord Jesus Christ.

Although his words and tone are formal, echoing the language of his era, they give us an earthy glimpse of both life in Tibet and his heart for and style of evangelism. His life and story laid a key part of the foundation for my father's life and, in turn, a key part of mine.

One of the most powerful tools that the Spirit of God uses to shape us as his outward-focused people is our family narrative. Each of us has a personal story to tell of stability or lack thereof, of grief and disappointment, of laughter or the resolve to never shed a tear, of the need to keep the peace, or the ingrained assumption that the world really is a good place. Perhaps alternative scenarios come to mind as you remember your own history. Some of our stories are happy, about relatively healthy families. Others of them are hard stories, filled with angry or absent parents, with fear or ancestor worship, with expectations or the longing for something else.

But God takes our gnarled narratives and reclaims them. He is an expert at redemption.

Story is a powerful tool for shaping, understanding and learning. Narrative provides detailed description, nuance and shading. 'Personal story can be like a trail', giving a 'sense of how and why the various parts of a life are connected and what gives the person meaning in life'.[1] Telling, reflecting on and examining our own life-accounts is 'essentially a meaning-making process',[2] helping us to identify God's formational work in us. After all, as one friend summarised, 'Understanding where we've been helps us know where we're going', or to paraphrase Søren Kierkegaard, life is understood backwards but lived forwards. Forming or telling stories helps, especially if your story is more reminiscent of a zigzag track – with detours, rocky terrain and varying levels of elevation along the way – than an unbending highway.

In his gentle and powerful book *The Pastor: A memoir*, Eugene Peterson ties together retrospective personal history and future vocation. He tells how his pastoral formation began in the family's shop run by his father, a butcher:

I am quite sure now that the way I as a pastor came to understand congregation had its beginnings in the 'congregational' atmosphere of our butcher shop. A church

. . . is a place where a person is named and greeted, whether implicitly or explicitly, in Jesus' name. A place where dignity is conferred. I first learned that under my father's priesthood in his butcher shop.[3]

I have been involved in global mission my whole life, from before my own story began. My grandparents served in mission in Asia and Africa respectively. On their return they married later in life and produced three children, the eldest of whom is my father. Our family left Australia when I was two and a half, hopping on a ship (yes, I am *that* old!) and sailing to the Philippines, where I spent the next eight and a half years. That has shaped me. It is a part of how I see and respond to the world, of how I understand God and follow after Jesus. I then, in turn, lived and served in Southeast Asia. It is a rich heritage, a wonderful story. But it also had an underbelly that I have bumped against over the years.

When I was in seminary, I took a course in which we examined our motivation for gospel involvement. Grace, gratitude, responsibility, biblical mandate, love and so on. Through our discussion, I realised that my motivation for involvement in global mission was responsibility. I bore a family duty to continue serving in mission, sharing the gospel with others. That semester, I asked the Lord to change my heart, reforming my motivation, letting it emerge from love, not the weight of obligation. He did. In the weeks that followed, he pursued me. I would wake to his presence each morning, and drop off to sleep each night, aware of his company. It was as if he met me after class, walking me to the next lecture. His presence was palpable, and I fell in love. I had loved him before, but it was during that semester that I fell *in love* with him.

But the bumping up against my story did not disappear with this holy romance. During my first few years in Southeast Asia, as I was learning the local language, I realised I had assumed I would learn it easily because I had grown up outside my home nation. Hmm . . .

not so. It was hard, and I was not a natural linguist, struggling with understanding the spoken word and the subtlety found in any language. I had foolishly believed the whispered encouragements of others about future possibilities or my trajectory, perhaps also succumbing to a sense of subconscious entitlement, as if those doors would automatically open because of my heritage. That is just ugly sin, in need of reshaping. Or it is lingering evidence of the lies the enemy sows and the false narratives we believe, for which we need healing. It is a hold the Lord has kindly released me from through prayer.

Some of you may be considering your own difficult family narrative, and wondering what can be redeemed from it, what good can come from such pain. When I led a session on this topic in Papua New Guinea, a man stood up, his face alight. He shared how his parents were both witch doctors. Now that he follows Jesus, he has realised that having this background has given him an acute sensitivity to the spirit world. God is using his refined spiritual discernment in his gospel witness.

Or I think about my own mother. Time and again friends will comment on how empathic she is, how she has an ability to listen to the said and unsaid. She asks gentle but probing questions that draw people out, and yet at the same time they know she is a safe space. She was entrusted with that gift through pain, though. She knows the confusion and anguish of losing her own mother at a young age, of being implanted into the immediate family of close relatives, and yet carrying around with her, the way a child carries a doll, that feeling of not quite belonging. She has known the deep desire to be accepted by her own nuclear siblings, and yet, because they did not share her faith, they held her at a distance. It is this experience of being an outsider that enables her to draw others in, to welcome them and create a place of belonging for them. This has been deepened and purified by the visceral, gut-level knowledge that she is embraced and loved by God. Others belong because she knows what it is like not to, and because she ultimately knows what it is to be grafted into her wider family of faith through the reforming work of the Spirit. She brings alive Ruth Haley Barton's words: 'There is something about being invited that makes the heart glad. Someone is seeking me out, desiring my presence enough to initiate an encounter.'[4] My mum, formed through her own family narrative, makes the hearts of others glad.

Another friend comes to mind. His background was rough, filled with trauma that was blocked out for years. Yet he has an uncanny ability to read others, to connect with those from different cultures by interpreting the gradation and shading of culture, of relationship. He fits in easily, an adapting chameleon, but completely genuine. When I heard his childhood story, of harsh words and hard fists, it made sense. He had to learn to read the atmosphere as a child, to interpret his stepfather's mood and pivot his behaviour accordingly. No wonder he can do that within a cultural context. Something that caused him to duck and shrink as a boy has given him gentle yet sharp acumen as a man. What a beautiful redemption of past pain. What a celebration of reclaimed history. It is a trail leading to the Master Artisan.

This kind of redemption emerges out of 'an increasingly faithful response to the One whose purpose shapes our path, whose grace redeems our detours, whose power liberates us . . . and whose transforming presence meets us at each turn in the road'.[5] This responsiveness, enlivened by the Spirit's touch, converts our family narrative into a dynamic avenue of formation into Christ's likeness, a meaningful outward witness.

Formation questions

1 Can you identify something from your family story – happy or hard – that is part of what has formed who you are?

2 Thinking about the quote 'Personal story can be like a trail', what meaningful trail does your personal narrative provide?

3 What can you celebrate, worshipping God for entrusting this part of your story to you for the sake of his greater story?

4 What do you keep bumping up against that needs reshaping?

5 How can God use your family story to bear witness to others?

6 Are you giving God permission to use your story for his purposes?

5

Formed from . . . influence

The impact of influential people

A while ago, friends I have known for years invited me to join them on their catamaran for just short of a week. Soon into our trip, we sailed overnight to an island on the southern rim of the Great Barrier Reef, Lady Musgrave Island. It is a small island, with an 8-kilometre (5-mile) circumference, surrounded by a turquoise lagoon which in turn is protected by a coral cay. It is where I first swam with green turtles. Oh, the wonder! But that is another story.

On our first morning there, Christine and I clambered on to 'stand-up paddle boards' (SUPs) and pushed off. The tidal current was strong, and we had to dig deep. I soon found myself on my knees to better control the board. We made it over to a patch of reef, with purples and blues staring up at us, small fish wiggling and flitting in and out of coral tunnels. At one stage I lay down on the board and plunged my goggle-covered face into the sea. An underwater world came into sharp focus, and only the shallow water stopped me from diving in. Pulling my head out of the water, I saw just how far I had quickly drifted. The current pulled at the board, and I scrambled to control its direction before I floated off too far.

When I reflect on the tug of influence that we have on one another's lives, it feels to me sometimes like the underwater drag of an ocean rip current, taking us to unexpected places. Other times it is more like gently marinating food, a spice that permeates and flavours. Gordon MacDonald, in *A Resilient Life*, encourages those he coaches to arrange their memories into three categories, one of which is: those significant people who have influenced us, leaving their mark, 'for good or ill'.[1] Does someone spring to mind, even as you read these words?

Who are the influential people in your life who have left their mark? Perhaps the mother who was the anchor of your family, the father who encouraged and believed in you, the spouse who taught you to love well, the teacher who gave you the gift of a new idea, the friend who was faithful and fun, the boss who empowered you, or the pastor who shepherded you with integrity and grace. Those who inspired or manipulated, encouraged or dissuaded, guided or induced, gave to or took from; those who have left their signature on our lives with care or callousness. Of course, our parents were or continue to be influential, whether by presence or absence. What about others? Teachers, pastors, leaders, friends, disciplers, mentors, coaches . . .? Who else has helped shape who you are today?

Ruth Wall, in explaining the influence that Jesus had on his disciples, writes:

> When Jesus trained his disciples he could not prepare them for every situation they would face or give them every tool to meet every challenge ahead. Instead, Jesus equipped his disciples for ministry through a change in their DNA. This is transformation. They were led through a process of transformation in their identity, worldview, attitudes, and relationships.[2]

Those who influence us, to large or small degrees, transform our identity, shade our worldview, affect our attitudes, shape our relationships. They infuse their influence into our history. Jesus did this in the most transformative and life-giving way. Through the Spirit, the process continues in each of us as we invite him in, submit to him and partner with him. Mysteriously, as he is a God who does not need to but loves to use his people to have an impact on others, the concentric circle of influence moves out in ever-increasing rings.

God has used Uncle JFK Mensah multiple times in my life, especially to mature my prayer life. After turbulent teenage years, this West African gave himself wholeheartedly to Jesus at the age of 18. At that time, Uncle JFK began to memorise Scripture in earnest. I mean, truly in earnest – a verse a day from Monday to Friday, review on Saturday and a rest on Sunday. Now in his sixties, when he preaches it is an artful weaving together of dozens and dozens of verses to build a point.

We rarely meet now, but when we met more regularly, perhaps once or twice a year, I would seek him out, perhaps sitting by him at a meal. 'Uncle JFK, what's the Lord teaching you at the moment?' I would ask. He would sit back, stretching out his long legs. 'Ah, Kaaaaate,' he would start, 'the Lord is teaching me to listen to him.' This is not only a wise man of God but also a prayerful man, walking in rhythm with the Spirit of God. Or he would say, 'The Lord is gathering me under his wing like a mother hen!' And he would fall into laughter, his joy spilling out like an overfull glass. It was in my night hours of prayer, however, that Uncle JFK had the most profound impact on me.

There was a group of us, a leadership cohort journeying together through a process of leadership development, with Uncle JFK as one of the facilitators. He was telling us about how he used wakeful night hours. For years he struggled with the health of his kidneys and so would wake up at least once in the early hours of the morning to make himself comfortable. He said: 'I would get back into bed and pray for a few minutes before falling asleep. Then I said to the Lord, "If you wake me up earlier, I will pray." So, he did, and I did.' He smiled. 'A few minutes before and after turned into a few hours of prayer.' These were precious times for him, when the world would still and those grabbing at him for input were silent. During those sacred hours he could listen and talk to the Lord undisturbed.

Over the years, I have been through seasons when I would wake up at 3 a.m. or so. There were times when I tossed and turned with increasing frustration, even anger at God for not helping me sleep: 'You are the God of all creation. You can help me sleep!' (I know, a bit like a petulant child.) But after hearing Uncle JFK's story, if I ever awoke in the still hours of the night, I would turn to prayer. Those wakeful periods are now irreplaceable minutes when the Spirit hovers and whispers clarity or ideas, when his presence is palpable with holy intimacy. It was during such a time that he led me to this very publisher – SPCK – a surprising and unexpected grace-gift on the opposite side of the globe.

Reena, my prayer partner for five years, is another person who has influenced me greatly. I think of how the Lord brought us together. Before leaving to live in Asia, I had begun praying for a local kindred spirit. Reena, thousands of miles away, was asking for God's provision of a prayer partner. Several years into my time in Southeast Asia, I had just emerged from a retreat, during which the Lord had encouraged me to get in touch with a handful of people. So, on this day, with the Spirit's nudging, I picked up the phone. Every year, on her birthday, Reena asks the Lord for something. This day happened to be her birthday, and my call was an answer to prayer. God, the great initiator, brought us together after many years, with a shared hope and a longing to pray deeply and widely in him. How else do you explain how two people from different continents, with different life-stories, going to different churches, located in different parts of a megacity of tens of millions of people, were drawn together as kindred spirits, heart sisters, prayer partners?

When I lived in this Asian urban centre, I would drive to her home, about thirty minutes away in those early years, and ninety minutes away in the latter years. We would talk and pray for hours, enjoying the thick, tangible unity of the Spirit. We were constantly surprised at how our similar although unique experiences of the previous weeks echoed similar although unique responses from the Lord, with him speaking to us personally and yet as partners in prayer. Through the fellowship of the Spirit, the hearts of two individuals were knitted together as one (echoing the unity of Philippians 2:2) to intercede for things heavy on God's heart.

Each year we would choose a theme and pray into it together. During those years, the Lord deepened both of our prayer lives in profound ways, using us both to speak into the lives of each other as true sisters in Christ. She is a rare gift, a *khushbu* – a pleasant scent, a sweet fragrance – a lasting influence on my life.

Who is your Uncle JFK? Your Reena? Who has been used by the Spirit to shape you towards himself over the years?

Influencers are not always light and life. A friend of mine, probably one of the most courageous people I know, did not grow up with parents who always loved him well, but he married someone who did love him dearly, and who wants the best for him. From time to time, I would meet up with them and he would process his work life. His boss was a person of contrasts – gentle and warm at times, but, with the suddenness of a flicked switch, a dark side would emerge. Fighting his own demons formed by his own haunted story, this man's dragon tail of anger would lash out with surprising force, with raw emotion and hurled words. However, he only displayed certain behaviours to certain people, and although it was not constant, my friend was one of the regular recipients of his hidden tirades, his Jekyll-and-Hyde turns. For some reason, my friend triggered his boss's 'feelings of inadequacy, insecurity, paranoia . . . touch[ing] some raw nerve'[3] of his. Although the hope is that our main leader of influence – be it our employer, direct report or the one with authority over us – would believe in and empower us, giving hope and meaningful encouragement while providing opportunities for development, it is not always the case. For my friend, his boss's unpredictability robbed him of a joyful and healthy workplace.

Who has stolen from you in this or similar ways? Did someone just dart across your mind?

But formed by the Spirit through adversity, my friend remains resilient and faithful and true, fulfilling his current vocation with dedication, wisdom and delicacy. He chooses to respond every time in kindness rather than harshness. Through Christ's renewing work in him, and knowing what it is to have someone's damaged side used as a weapon against him, he enables others to recognise their own brokenness so that it can be 'redeemed and restored'.[4]

As God's people we can reclaim the influence others have had or continue to have on our lives. In the same way that I display a certain family likeness to my parents, I long to reflect the Father's family likeness through the reshaping he has done in my life. In turn, this allows me – us – to influence others in a way that looks like Jesus. 'You're looking more like your mum the older you get,' my cousin told me the last time I saw him. It made me smile with love for her. More than anything, though, I want to look like Jesus, with his spiritual genes and DNA forming me into who I am today, colouring my life as I seek to walk alongside others, spilling out onto them in Jesus-shaded ways.

Formation questions

1 As you consider those who have influenced your life, what can you celebrate? What has brought sadness, discouragement or harm, and needs to be grieved?
2 How has God redeemed people's harmful impact on your life, or changed your story?
3 How has the Lord enabled you to help others redeem their stories?
4 Where would you like to see further change in your life, deepening the formation work God has already done?
5 If there was one family likeness – Christlike DNA, so to speak – that you would want to pass on to others, what would it be?
6 Whom do you need to seek out as a godly influence in your life?

6

Formed from . . . pain

The mysterious etchings of suffering

In mid-May 2021, Covid-19 was peaking in one of the most populous countries in Asia, gathering thousands each day in the swing of its grim-reaper scythe. An overhead drone captured hundreds of smouldering funeral pyres, each a sign of a soul lost, a family grieving. During those weeks I was chatting with some dear friends. Thomas, a pastor, was exhausted, wrung out from lovingly and faithfully caring for his people. His wife, Raina, a respected doctor, was stepping into each day with fortitude, leading her team and caring for patients as best she could, knowing that options were limited. Soon after, I received a link, this time for a funeral service of another friend's father who had passed away. When I pressed on the link, the service was ending. It was surreal, a portal to another world with figures clad in full-body personal protective equipment, moving in seemingly slow motion. A handful of people shifted to the burial plot, red earth heaped high, and the coffin was lowered. Although he was a Christian, sure of never-ending life with Jesus, sorrow hovered thick. The suffering was real.

Scripture gives us a range of glimpses into suffering. We can jump to the often-used example of Job, but what of others? There are a multitude of individuals who brought pain on themselves and others through their own unwise choices. Adam and Eve provide Scripture's first example, their decision exiling them from 'walking [with God] in the garden in the cool of the day' (Genesis 3:8 NIV). Moving through the history of God's people, consider the anguish that Moses must have felt at not entering the promised land after leading the Israelites for so long. In a moment, he struck a rock instead of speaking to it, dishonouring and breaking trust with God in front of the whole community (Numbers 20:12). Because of that, the boundary was drawn. He would not see the fruit of his life's work leading God's people. Or think about King David, who made one bad decision after another, culminating in the loss of a child he had with a woman stolen from her husband. This hardship continued through the learned behaviour of his children. Or contemplate the complaining Jonah, who was tossed overboard in a storm, ending up in the slimy centre of an ocean creature. Not a pleasant experience, but avoidable if he had made different choices. Or ponder the disciple Peter, in terrible grief at having denied the one who had irrevocably changed his life.

Often, though, pain and suffering come at the hands of others. Leah and Jacob's daughter, Dinah, was violated because the local ruler's son fell for her. Genesis 34 speaks of her brothers being 'shocked and furious' (v. 7), but what of her own anger and grief? What of her shame? Or remember Joseph. What was it like for him to be assaulted by his brothers and left to die? Or later, going to prison through no fault of his own? He found favour in jail, and emerged well from those years, but did he ever have days of despair, wondering if that was it? What was it like for Esther to be at the beck and call of a megalomaniac? What was it like for Mary and Joseph? Although sure of the precious nature of the child Mary carried, did they feel shame or loneliness when people avoided eye contact, or wondered at their sanity? How did their local community respond?

Then, of course, there is the suffering and harm that comes to those who wholeheartedly follow God and his Son, Jesus. Suffering, that, if they compromised, would not come their way. Someone such as the prophet Hosea, who obediently married a woman who consistently gave herself to other men so that he could live out the story of Israel's unfaithfulness to God in living colour. Did Hosea have days when he just sat and wept, hot tears of sorrow, longing for a wife who wanted no one but him? Or what of his children, who grew up with names that spoke of punishment and lost love and shattered covenant relationship? Skipping to the New Testament, what of the narrative of Paul and Silas in Acts 16? Because they brought wholeness to a girl drowning in spirits, they were jailed. We often remember that this story is marked by their fortitude, expressed through song and prayer. But how easy it is to forget that their backs were in strips after receiving a severe flogging, and they were surely in intense pain, their feet secured in stocks. Suffering came because they followed fast after Christ and sought to share him in that moment, with that young female slave, among that crowd. They did not sink into despondency. Instead, they turned this story into a Christ-focused story, bearing witness to God as the other prisoners listened, and finally, as the jailer sought to take his own life. Suffering and witness were linked together as they supernaturally – because it certainly was not a human response – celebrated their suffering so that others could '[b]elieve in the Lord Jesus' (Acts 16:31).

We do not always think about the role of suffering in shaping us into Christlikeness for the sake of other people. Yet it is one of God's sacred tools for shaping, although it often leaves impressions, scars or theology split apart, lying on the ground like a dry coconut husk. It can soften us, though, maturing our empathy, expanding our perspective and faith. It can bear witness. Most experiences of pain are communal, shared with a constellation of often unknown others, while each ache remains severely individual – such as the ache of a dorm mate who was abused, or a colleague who lost one unborn child after another, or a friend whose spouse painted both of their worlds grey through a wrestle with mental health issues. It is a tender idea to consider – the part deep hurt plays in shaping us – a callous or tender tool in our formation, depending on our perspective. I am convinced that those who have gone through suffering see the world with deeper dimension, noticing the concealed, the camouflaged, when most look past it. Their lived experience adds layers, and often wisdom, to their contribution.

Frederick Buechner, one of my favourite authors, talks about 'stewarding' our pain. We can ignore it. We can be trapped in it. Or we can see it as something delicate God has entrusted to us, for us to hold carefully, tenderly. It is part of our call to be a people of hope and faith. Buechner expands this thought:

> Being a good steward of your pain involves . . . being alive to your life. It involves taking the risk of being open, of reaching out, of keeping in touch with the pain as well as the joy of what happens because at no time more than at a painful time do we live out of the depths of who we are instead of out of the shallows.[1]

How we respond to hurt, pain, trauma, suffering, ache, loss, grief and so on either aligns us with the sufferings of Christ, giving us a rare glimpse into that sacred part of his earthly journey, or pulls us away. We can gently hold and steward our pain, perhaps feeling off-kilter at first, and then more comfortable with this new reality, offering it back up to God for his redemptive use. Ajith Fernando reminds us that there is a powerful level of unity with Christ that can only come via the avenue of suffering. He goes on to ask: 'What if our greatest desire in life is to get close to Jesus and we recognize that suffering will help us achieve our ambition?'[2]

One family brings this to life for me. Their first child was born with a severe disability, not expected to survive her first year. Her condition was 'not conducive to life', they were told, words no parent wants to hear. Ainhoa, however, defied expectation. While her disability meant she was unable to communicate verbally and needed assistance with each aspect of her daily routine, tucked into a wheelchair for mobility, Ainhoa lived a full and varied life for eighteen years. This family longed to serve overseas in global mission, living gospel lives as a beautiful yet uncommon household in another nation, every single member a part of fulfilling God's missional invitation to them. But what mission organisation would be crazy enough to say yes to a family with a child with such intense and complex needs? An impediment, or a gift? Ainhoa was indeed a gift. You see, Ainhoa was the hub of the family as they all served in mission. Full of joy and love, she drew people into their community, into the good, good story they told of Jesus. Through this family's love for Ainhoa and her love for them, through their honouring of this precious daughter and her response to them, those around them witnessed the grace and love of Jesus. She was an integral part of how they did mission together. Ainhoa died in late 2017 while embedded in her family as they lived gospel lives outside Australia. The pain and grief continue for this family, but it looks so different now. A hole, a visceral missing of someone deeply loved, a part of the whole now gone. I wonder: is it anything like how the Father missed the Son for those days of his death?

Some time ago I saw a post from Ainhoa's mum on social media. She wrote of a different anguish, a distinctly other loss. By now the related ache had changed shape – this particular darkness being tinged with light, this particular sadness accompanied by hope:

Light . . . Do you see it? For . . . years, I have felt that every step I have taken in following God has led me further . . . into the darkness until I could no longer see the light, but it doesn't mean it wasn't there. As it says in Genesis 1:2–4, 'Now the earth was formless and empty, darkness was over the surface of the deep, and the spirit of God was hovering over the waters. And God said, "Let there be light." God saw that the light was good, and he separated the light from the darkness.' The light was in the darkness, and it was good, before God separated them. Just because I can't see it doesn't mean it isn't there and it isn't good.

Her faith and hope, and yet her vulnerability in admitting that, yes, there is sadness and incomparable loss which has touched her, bears powerful witness to how heavily she is leaning on this God of light who remains good, even amid pain.

'Pain is a tragedy,' writes Larry Crabb. 'But it's never only a tragedy. For the Christian, it's always a necessary mile on the long journey to joy.'[3] It is the reformation of suffering, the reshaping of pain supernaturally into something else.

Yumba is another who comes to mind. Originally from Congo-Kinshasa, he escaped the terrible warfare there only to be trapped in a Zambian refugee camp for fifteen or so years. This would send some into despair, but instead Yumba told others about Jesus and gathered those people into churches. Finally able to migrate to Australia, he is now being used by God to minister to refugees who have gone through trauma. Part of Yumba's story is shaped by deep distress and suffering, but it does not define him. It was a part of his formation but is not his identity. Instead, he stewards it as an offering to God and a blessing to others. Like the red ground rose I severely prune each winter, but now overflows with flowering buds, he too embodies new life out of hurt. It is as if the shed blood of Christ crucified acts as a fertiliser, rich with nutrients to bring life. It is so much more than this, but it is no less either.

At times it is difficult for some of us in resource-rich nations to be able to identify with certain experiences of hardship. In some ways the worldwide shared experience of Covid closed the gap around suffering. Most people struggled in one way or another, although these experiences were many and varied. They were variables of loss. Loss of life, loss of business and livelihood, loss of sanity, loss of health, loss of love and opportunity and freedom. Loss of security. Loss of the world as we knew it. Loss on so many levels. Although we cannot equate the thousands of funeral pyres in India or the around-the-clock digging of graves in Brazil with being in lockdown for several months and struggling with profound loneliness, we do know that domestic abuse spiked during that time – a different, angry face of Covid. Loss of another kind; ache in another form.

As we began to emerge from the pandemic, commentators were arguing over whether we should plan to simply step back into pre-Covid life when able to. But would that not have rejected the lessons learned? Lessons about how to consolidate or reform our theology to embrace suffering for those with an unformed theology of suffering. Lessons about how to not just endure, but practise resilience, even joyful resilience. Lessons about not running from the emotions of sadness, despondency, grief or hopelessness, but instead looking them in the face and walking through the dark tunnel, hand in hand with the God who knows darkness, and waiting to emerge out the other side. Are those lessons not worth learning and integrating? Do they not deepen us as God's people? Do they not help us authentically live out the call and invitation of Romans 5:3–5,[4] with the domino effect of trials developing endurance, which bumps against and moves into motion character and, in turn, hope, enlivened by God the Spirit, committedly at work within us?

In my last job, I was involved for many years in preparing mission workers for cross-cultural life and service. Along with the broader team, we always struggled with how to impart lessons around pain, how to mature someone's theology of suffering. People cognitively understand this, but it is a piece often missing in integration and application within our context. Then Covid came along. Plans were put on hold. Mission workers wrestled with a drop in financial support as businesses shut and many failed economically. Families and churches and friends doubted their resolve. Their theology was tested; their relationship with God was tried through lockdown and loss. They had to grapple genuinely with the role of hardship and suffering in their life. They had to embrace the chaos, the doubt, the unknowns, the grief, the pain, the surprising responses that would suddenly arise, revealing the ugliness of their sin. They had to make their peace with it all, further trusting God in raw and profound ways. This kind of learning cannot be replaced. If it is stewarded well, they will have learned more of the suffering of Christ, and it will shade and enrich their future ministries exponentially. After all, '[t]here are no shortcuts to developing depth. If you want to have a deep impact on this world, you will have to suffer.'[5] Stewarding suffering for missional purposes is a tender privilege, a sacred trust.

Jeremiah once received a message from God to go down to the local potter's shop. The prophet says: 'So I did as he told me and found the potter working at his wheel. But the jar he was making did not turn out as he had hoped, so he crushed it into a lump of clay again and started over' (Jeremiah 18:3–4). Suffering feels like that at times, as if the God of all creation and redemption has reached down and caught hold of us, squashing the clay of our lives into a lump, reducing us, diminishing us, breaking us. Those words may come to mind when we are viewing our lives through the lens of self, orientating our world around ourselves as the centrepiece, rather than around Jesus as the focus. We desire his glory but hesitate if it is at our expense or if it comes at a cost too high. We ignore or forget how gentle his hands are, how he moistens the clay with water to rework our lives. We forget how he is a skilled artist, a trustworthy God who knows exactly what the result is that he is working towards. For, as Tiffany Clark reminds us: 'In God's story, death ends in resurrection. Sorrow ends in comfort. Shame ends in glory. Brokenness ends in renewal. And suffering ends in redemption.'[6]

Formation questions

1 Consider your own journey of suffering. What pain and suffering in your life has formed you, and how?

2 If your past hurt or hardship defines you, what steps can you take to seek help in reforming your identity?

3 Has pain allowed you to draw closer to Jesus, or has it driven a wedge between you, creating distance? If so, how?

4 How has suffering added depth to you?

5 When have you noticed the gentleness of God's hands as he has formed you through hardship?

6 How are you able to steward your pain and suffering as an offering to God and a blessing to others?

7

Formed from . . . gift-mix

Entrusted grace-gifts

I first met Kaye many years ago. She is quiet and gentle-natured. An artist, I heard. 'Oh, that's interesting,' I thought, tucking away this bit of information. It was not long, though, before I was swept away by her art, its unique style telling stories. Every time I visit my cousin, I am reminded of Kaye's gifting once again as I gaze at a piece hanging on the living-room wall. In the biography on her previous website, she wrote of being an artist and creative educator, her hands messy with paint from an early age. Kaye's love of travel motivated her to draw. It fuelled her artistry. 'Being an artist has literally opened up the world to me,' she wrote. 'I feel so privileged to be able to use my gift to share my faith and heart with people from all different cultures, languages and backgrounds.'[1] Now art itself has become the main avenue for storytelling in a way that surpasses language. 'My work holds much spiritual significance while telling stories with careful attention to the tangible world around me,' she explained. It is a vehicle for faith-sharing in a way that moves people in subterranean places, of identification with others, regardless of culture or background.

Are we formed through our gift-mix as opportunity presents and passion motivates, or do we shape it? This is an interesting question to consider. 'Picasso understood that . . . the one who creates is also in a sense being created . . . we are being informed and formed long before we begin to express ourselves.'[2] And so it is. We are readied to step into using our gift-mix, but we are also, in a coinciding manner, repeatedly formed by using our gift-mix, like a favourite play list on repeat, the ever-present Spirit hovering, guiding, shaping.

What is meant exactly by 'gift-mix'? I use this term because it is more than just our spiritual gifts. It is a mix of all kinds of gifts, passions, hobbies and loves that God has awakened in us to bring him glory and us joy.

Gift-mix includes our spiritual gifts, of course.[3] As we step into the grace-gifts imparted to us by God the Spirit, we are formed. As we learn and fail, or try and fumble, we are moulded. Not just our skills, but our character, the wedding partner of skill. Do we preach as though the word of God has changed our life, or as though it was an intellectual exercise? Do we entertain with true welcome or with strict limits? Do we weigh our wisdom with empathy, or speak it to prove a point or win a battle? Do we remember, as we move ahead with these gifts, that they have been entrusted to us from another source, and that we are to hold them humbly, to practise them in partnership with the Spirit? In his book *The Pastor*, Eugene Peterson tells of how he had always written, but how it was through his wilderness experience of congregational malaise, which he calls 'the Badlands', that he became a writer. An ability turned on the wheel of vocation, transformed from words written to words that breathed life.

The starting point for all of this is the grace we have received; grace from Christ – through his work on the cross and through the Spirit's continued work of building our character and nature into his likeness – and the gifts he has poured out on us, as we see in 1 Corinthians 12:8.[4] I like how the New International Version draws out this idea of grace, as Paul reminds us in another letter: 'to each one of us grace has been given as Christ apportioned it' (Ephesians 4:7 NIV). We *have* because we have *been given*. Both our salvation and the spiritual gifts and abilities we have to serve with are grace-given. Or as Paul again reminds us: 'We have different gifts, according to the grace given to each of us' (Romans 12:6 NIV). Put another way, we have different *charismata* (the same Greek term used in 1 Corinthians 12:9) according to the *charis* (grace) given to each of us. The apostle Peter urges us: 'use whatever gift you have received to serve others, as faithful stewards of God's grace in its various forms' (1 Peter 4:10 NIV). These gifts and grace are linked. What we have termed 'spiritual gifts' can just as easily be termed 'grace-gifts'. God's grace-gifts to us, offered freely and generously, given as we minister to one another in mutuality.

The Father also delights in taking and using other parts of who we are. He is not limited to the lists in the Scripture passages above, written for the explicit building up of his church.

In his book *Windows of the Soul*, Ken Gire writes of how '[w]e long for the companionship of God',[5] and how he can use a range of pathways to lead us there. Gire's chapters focus on a range of topics: stories, art, poetry, films, writing, nature, and a list of others. There is something that draws us to those listed above – an interest, an ability, a passion. Through an iterative, recurring process, we are pulled towards them; we seek out opportunities to enjoy them as hobbies or pursuits. They influence and form us, while at the same time we can be developing an ability that orbits around these same passions. These, then, if offered up to God revealed in Christ, can be grafted into our holy jumble of gifts that point others to him.

Anjelita, from South America, models the use of our gift-mix with passion and faithfulness. She is a trauma counsellor, but she also loves gardening. An idea took root – and a vegetable plot took shape, expanding over time to become a garden. This green space was built for refugees wrestling with mental health issues because of the trauma that stalked them from their birth nation, stowing away on their flight from danger. The aim was to create a safe space, a place of belonging and nurture, to help them find restoration in the secure harbour of Jesus and his people. Anjelita will give a lesson about gardening, weaving biblical truths and support for their mental health through her narrative. God the great gardener has developed her interest in cultivating for his kingdom purposes. As she digs her hands into the soil, she is filled and spills out to others. Together with her team, she has formed a place of welcome and growth and healing, a literal and metaphorical plot of land to sow and grow herbs and hope, corn and kindness, tomatoes and tenacity, the roots of resilience going deep.

When the organisation I am a part of first started, it gained a reputation (and not always a kind one) for accepting anyone as a mission worker. Although this was not true, it can at times have more flexibility than some other organisations. A part of this equation, though, is that the initial founders recognised God at work through non-traditional means. They saw strength in people with creative ideas and innovative methods: owners of a mountain bike or scuba business; writers or media specialists; crafters of jewellery; bakers; individuals with passions and interests bridging the divide to others who do not know Jesus but have these same interests. As these passions, interests or hobbies are explored and enjoyed, they shape us, giving us a deeper sense of God's creativity and world, gifting us with a sense of the Spirit at work as God's mission in the world is expressed in a million ways.

Photography has been a passion of mine for years. I got my first camera – a second-hand film-based, classic 'wind and shoot' SLR (single-lens reflex) model – when I was 18, and slowly built up a collection of lenses, eventually switching it for a digital camera. I was able to use that skill as part of my business platform while living in South Asia, creating gift cards. It allowed me to communicate with hundreds of people over the years, bringing stories and people to life through visual means. What I have loved most about it, though, is that when I am out taking photos, it is as if the Spirit of God is palpably close, draping his presence over me as I marvel at and capture glimpses of the world. Those times have formed me, nurturing a sense of awe, refining the ability to pay attention, to be filled with joy at the smallest glimpse of the Creator's signature. This paying-attention leads to worship. It is a filling-up of sorts. It is an opportunity to frame colour, wonder and life, as the unexpected, interesting or organic flits across my path.

As we take these grace-gifts and offer them to others, we bring glory to God and blessing to others. Springboarding off Marilynne Robinson's wonderful quote 'you have been God's grace to me' in her novel *Gilead*,[6] Christine Pohl writes:

> Hearing from another person that 'you have been God's grace to me' changes how we experience the ordinariness of our lives and the sacrifices we willingly make for the good of others. Seeing ourselves and others as expressions or embodiments of God's grace transforms life together. It simultaneously recognizes God's goodness and the ways in which we have been gifted through other persons.[7]

I have those words, 'You have been God's grace to me', written on a back window at home. It is a reminder of the cascading flow of God's good gifts. He is the source, pouring himself out to us with his grace-gifts. We receive them, blended and fused together through the work of the Spirit, and in turn pour them out as God's grace-gifts to others. It is an outward expression of living as Jesus-shaped people.

Formation questions

1 Reflect on your mix of gifts. What do you identify?
2 What are the spiritual gifts that have formed you, or the hobbies that have shaped you?
3 What has helped you nurture a sense of wonder and worship?
4 How has your character become more like Christ's as you have grown in your gift-mix?
5 Are there parts of the person God has made you to be that you have not woven into your gift-mix?
6 Do you need help in identifying other passions, interests, hobbies or gifts, or help in combining them together in your gift-mix? If so, seek out some wise counsel.

8

Formed from . . . learning

The lessons of education, learning and unlearning

We stood in her kitchen, enjoying the full-bodied aroma of fried onion and garlic ready to be thrown into the awaiting *kardai* chicken and *dal makhani*. We had been chatting for a while, catching up on the months since we had last spent time together. Rolling out the dough for chapatis, she turned to me and asked, 'What is the Lord teaching you at the moment?' This was years before I had learned to ask this question myself. No one had asked me anything quite like that before. I liked it. Penetrating questions such as this point lifelong learners to the greatest, most patient teacher the world has ever known: the One whose teaching methods are broad and blended, creative and often unexpected. Ever since that conversation, my friend's question has been a constant help to me. I find myself praying: 'Lord, what do you want me to learn through this experience, or that person? How might I grow into your likeness in this aspect of my life? What are you teaching me?' And I have found myself echoing her question to others.

It is easy to make assumptions about how we are formed through education. We are shaped by the knowledge we receive as we study, whether it be medicine or media, theology or farming, accounting or the arts. We are also conditioned through the very system of education we emerge from. We may have received a state/public or private education; extracurricular involvement may or may not have been available, expected or celebrated. Our cultural background may have included rote learning; perhaps questions were discouraged, or perhaps they were valued. Either logic or intuition may have been nurtured. Engagement in lively discussions, or respectful waiting to speak; reading or watching; shame-based or encouragement-based learning – any of these may have been a part of the learning process. Knowledge influences us, but so does the system of learning.

Growing up in a Western educational system, I came to appreciate asking questions as a method for learning. I love hearing stories of what others are learning. I value learning from and with others. And I have the spiritual gift of rambling(!), enjoying how words can express a thought, a swirl of imagination or an idea. So, speaking comes easily to me, perhaps too easily, a confidence developed by being on the debating team at school and growing up in a ministry family. This is part of what has formed me, part of what I can gift to others. But it is also part of what I need to unlearn.

Working in an international organisation means that I have a rich exposure to people from cultures other than my own. You notice things – who remains quiet and who speaks too much within any given discussion, whose counsel causes others to pause and reflect, and whose is swallowed in the ping-pong match of commentary. You observe who hears what is left unsaid as well as what is stated clearly, and who hears only the explicit. You witness who speaks with their mouth and who speaks with their whole self, who understands the subtle nuances of the latter – 'reading the air', as Erin Meyer calls it in *The Culture Map*, quoting a Japanese colleague[1] – and who misses it completely.

The process of unlearning the habit of constantly asking questions, satiating an enquiring mind, or speaking quickly is a lifelong one. I have a very, very, very long way to go. Prompts from Siang-Yang Tan and Douglas Gregg unsettle me, reminding me to value attentive listening:

Choose to listen to others around you before you speak. This involves consciously and continuously checking in with God before you respond, and deliberately evaluating your intended speech to see if what you are about to say is really worth saying at all. By practicing silence this way in the midst of everyday life, you will come to realize that many of your words are only chaff. Silence gives the Holy Spirit an opportunity to sow his thoughts in your mind and heart![2]

I appreciate how Tan and Gregg are encouraging not just silence but also attentiveness to God the Spirit. By listening to his voice above other voices, we prioritise his voice as most important, most authoritative. What is the Spirit saying? How can you express *that* thought? But in reality, his voice often gets drowned out in the busyness of discussion.

One respected leader and colleague comes to mind. He is good at this kind of intentional listening; waiting, weighing his words so that when he does speak, he is worth listening to. Listening is a precious and powerful gift to others. It 'is a kindness we can give to others in a self-obsessed world where very few people are heard deeply enough to feel understood'.[3] For many of us, it will be a process of lifelong learning to refine the gift of listening well to the said and the unsaid. It will be a process of Spirit-dependent death, for '[d]ying to self by listening for as long as it takes is an act of grace made possible only by leaning on God's grace'.[4]

It is truly a learned skill to listen well, to invite others to share their story and remain silent long enough for them to leave your presence feeling that bit more known. I have spent weeks with people and left them no more personally known than when I arrived. I do not want to make that mistake with others, to miss out on the mutual gift of knowing and being known. For true learning is limited if it involves only the accumulation of cognitive knowledge. It is richest if it includes the tender collection of stories where we refine the skill of knowing others and learning from them.

We are profoundly formed by those from whom we learn, but we are also shaped by those with whom we learn. Having a best friend at school whose cultural background is different from our own opens our world. Studying alongside those who are a decade or generation older than us informs our perspective. Being bullied can steal a sense of self-worth or give us an inner strength beyond our years.

The seminary that I first attended was tucked away in the winding hills of a southern state in the USA. It was a classic seminary experience – campus-based, classroom-grounded, structured. My time there expanded my world. It is where I fell in love with Jesus in a life-changing way. Fifteen and a half years later I entered my second seminary experience. Different in every way, this time the lecturer came to us – an American reminiscent of the professor in the film *Back to the Future*. The 'us' consisted of a small multicultural doctoral cohort located in the Pacific region: three men from Papua New Guinea, a Māori man from New Zealand, a British guy located in Australia, and me, the sole woman.

Of course, we were all formed by what we learned, our communal deep probing into varied subject-matter, and through the discipline and privileged sacrifice of those four years. However, it was this collection of worldwide brothers for which I am most grateful. Jay's study was around the 'Mutuality of Belonging'. Yet we all grew as we observed him gingerly stepping into the canoe of his Māori heritage, taking up the oar and learning to row with growing confidence as he came to belong to a people he had been separated from in his youth. Unia's enquiry into the Melanesian idea of *gutpela sindaun* (spiritual and material wholeness), as it links with the biblical concept of *shalom* and applies to his local Papua New Guinean context, was fascinating. But in addition to this learning, our whole cohort also saw a supreme anthropologist at work in his strategic thinking, his methodology and the communication of his ideas. More than that, we witnessed this unassuming, gracious man live out precise methodology within a communal culture, respecting elders, listening to the whole as well as individuals. Amos, also from Papua New Guinea, taught us about the positive impact, richness and challenges of the *wantok* system – a kinship-based structure of communal sharing and reciprocity. He also modelled for us how to engage in valuable, non-linear thinking while grappling with a subject and deliberating deeply on it. David, our sole Brit (although living in the Oceania region), circled his research around 'Relocating Holism' within a mission sphere that is very specific about its understanding of mission. His gift for teaching God's word or a concept, his choice of expression, his humble stance of wrestling with a topic and honouring his organisation displayed not only a sharp mind but also a genuine love for and commitment to his community. Julian, our third brother from Papua New Guinea, opened another aspect of the spirit world to us while graciously and gracefully holding in tension his role as a full-time pastor of an urban church. Finally, from our lecturer and leader, Dr Shaw, I not only learned how to read more broadly, probe more deeply, analyse more precisely and write more clearly; I also learned how to live life with passion and fullness, joy and curiosity – regardless of age.

It is this characteristic of curiosity that is essential to lifelong learning and the consequent formation that occurs with it. There seem to be two kinds of people: those who retain curiosity and those who, whether through intention or not, have shut it down. They have given up being intrigued or wondering or being teachable. There are many reasons for this kind of mental or emotional stalling, where people 'lock up the heart and seal off feelings . . . keeping things easy and comfortable . . . valu[ing] all-knowing over always learning and staying curious'.[5] It may be related to a lack of self-awareness, or a deep weariness, or perhaps the root end of a pain tucked away so deep and out of the way that they do not want it to see the light. That is when we need holy courage to step into the uncomfortable. It allows us to begin unlearning the unhealthy lessons of life and embrace new ideas, habits and rhythms with fellow sojourners who value not always knowing or understanding, and who are curious enough to explore mysteries, big and small.

God can use anything to shape and deepen us in him, to grow us up into his likeness. Valuing and retaining an open attitude to learn, a teachable spirit to discover and grow, and a holy curiosity sets us up well for this. Then we can take the system or context we are in, the content we are studying, along with our community of learners. We can explore it all like a prism held to the light, the various lessons, gifted by the Holy Spirit, shining out with refracted colour. For as we learn, we see that the Spirit's methods of shaping are broad and creative. He uses all of life to mould us for his mission among all peoples.

> He uses the evils we face, the people we can't stand, the circumstances of tension and pressure, the tedium of long afternoons, the solicitations of compromise, the irritations of angry customers, the interruptions, the financial reversals, the deals that fall through, even the traffic on the way home – He uses all of it to make us like Jesus.[6]

At times we forget what it means to be a disciple. At its simplest, it means being a student, a learner. As disciples – learners – of Christ, our classroom is everywhere – our marriage and family, work or church, our neighbourhood or local pub, the geopolitical situation, what we watch, read or listen to. The list goes on. God uses it all so that he can refine us into those who exude Jesus to those with whom he has invited us to cross paths.

Formation questions

1 Pause for a moment to consider how the content and system of your education has formed you.
2 Think about the people you studied with. How have they influenced you?
3 What abiding lessons have you learned from school or university friends and fellow students?
4 What do you need to unlearn?
5 Has your lifelong learning grown sedentary? If so, how can you proactively nurture the posture of lifelong learning?
6 What is the Lord presently teaching you?

9

Formed from . . . culture

The unique seasoning that culture brings

Using your holy imagination, can you see that vast, multicoloured crowd of Revelation 7:9–10 stretching into the distance? Perhaps under the white robes mentioned in verse 9 will be sea-green saris and tribal woven skirts, batik shirts and Ghanaian head wraps. Holding the palm branches will be hands with olive, beige and cocoa skin. There may be instruments scattered throughout this crowd: djembes and tablas, sitars and pan flutes, jazz pianos and egg shakers, didgeridoos and *cajón* drum boxes. It is a constellation of people shaped by culture. From the back, a 'Mexican wave' of worship sweeps through the crowd: 'King Jesus, the Lamb, Saviour!' This mass of believers is one in its worship. It is grand, full of multicultural, loud, Jesus-focused worship, and it is good! Can you see it?

For many of us who love God's word and desire to live out his heart for the nations, these are verses that inspire us. They motivate us towards becoming a unified, diverse, respectful, celebratory, multicultural, outward-focused gospel community, where enjoying one another and working together is itself a strategy for God's mission in the world. There is the weighty knowledge that we are less without the richness of other cultures beside our own.

We are all formed by culture: the culture of our nation, our family, our generation, the culture or subculture of our socio-economic position. Those of us who are 'third-culture kids or adults', that is, people who have lived a portion of their lives outside their parents' passport nations, or cross-cultural kids who have 'lived in – or meaningfully interacted with – two or more cultural environments for a significant period of time during development years',[1] are shaped by an intersection of cultures. On it goes. Our culture shapes our theology (whether we want to admit it or not); it has an impact on how we receive a passing comment or gesture. It moulds our responses, what we value, how we desire to live team life or outwardly express God's mission here on earth, how we pray and worship, disciple others and live family life. Much of it is good; some of it is bad, warped by sin and brokenness. Because each culture is different, we each have something to offer the other; a mutual exchange of gifts, one to the other. More so, we need this mutuality. Without this exchange, life is less; we are less. Arguable though it may be, dare I say it, our gospel witness can be diminished. Because when the fullness of the body of Christ – including cultural diversity – is working well, that bears witness, and Jesus is honoured.

As conversations around culture and racism have intensified through the Black Lives Matter movement, it is not unusual to hear a light-skinned person defend themselves by saying, 'I don't see them as black', or 'Their culture doesn't matter to me', meaning it as an expression of friendship or identification. But culture does matter. Skin colour does matter, because it is part of the intricate story we have to offer others. It is not racist to say, 'I see that you are Anglo-French, Chinese, Kenyan, Palestinian, Latino or Aboriginal Australian.' It is racist to see people as either diminished or superior because of those aspects of who they are, aspects that are only part of the whole. Those elements in themselves and what they represent can add to the rich tapestry of their lives; they can be a gift. If we close our eyes to those parts of a person, it does not make us culturally mature; it simply makes us blind.

Biased attitudes of being more or less, however, do not always emerge from external sources. After reading this book through, my Asian pastor, who has experienced the spectrum of cultural privilege and prejudice, shared the following with me. Sometimes we are diminished by others because of our culture or skin colour. At other times, though, we see ourselves as less, with a sense of inferiority creeping in and burrowing deep. It is prejudice or racism but of a different kind. This time the perpetrator emerges from an internal place rather than solely from external influences, with the victim wholeheartedly believing the lies that leave them diminished.

Recognising the complexity and continuum of these stories and realities, how we can intentionally ask, with our whole lives: 'I see that you are or I am [fill in the appropriate ethnicity here]. What can we recognise of the beauty and brokenness within our various cultures? What can I learn from you, and you from me, in this mutual exchange? Most importantly, how can we become more like Jesus together?'

There is much we can learn from one another through culture, and so be shaped by it. When we are immersed in or bump up against another culture, it enlarges us, giving us a broader insight into who God is. It expands our capacity to relate to and communicate with those who see the world differently from us. It invites us into the full embrace of the global, multicultural body of Christ that stretches across the centuries and across the seas and across time into eternity. Gifting others with how we have been shaped can be relational gold.

I remember teasing Uncle Fred, a well-loved, well-respected Ghanaian man I have known for decades, as we sat in the back of a conference room where a leadership development session was running. He was about to be interviewed regarding the reality and progress of multiculturalism within our organisation. Leaning over with a smile on his face, he whispered, 'What should I talk about?' 'Do a dance,' I quietly laughed, an absurd suggestion and made in pure fun. 'OK,' he answered, a mischievous twinkle in his eye.

Towards the end of the interview, after giving insightful responses to several questions, he looked at me and smiled. 'In West Africa we have a dance. There are about four or five drums, small drums, all kinds of drums. But there is a big one, and you have to listen to the big one, because the big one gives you the green light to start moving into the circle. So, you stand at the edge, and then you are warming up as others are dancing, but you wait for the big drum.' He began to dance with the smooth, funky rhythm that often flows when Africans dance. 'As soon as you hear the drumbeat, it means "Come on – get into the middle."' At this stage, Uncle Fred grabbed an American guy sitting at the front, who tried and failed to dance with finesse, much to the room's enjoyment.

'As I was growing up,' Uncle Fred continued, 'nobody told me that as you came into the circle you should stay there for two minutes, or three minutes. You have to discern that there are others warming up at the edge. So, you and I' – he pointed to the American guy still with him – 'we display our skills, but we don't have to stay here for too long. We move back. When we don't move back, to our shame you see that another set of people, they are coming into the circle. It means we have overstayed, and we have to find our way back shamefully.'

Uncle Fred began to sway to a silent beat again. 'I wasn't thinking about that before, but when we think about dance, I think about the dance of the Trinity, where the Father, Son and Holy Spirit . . . there's a dance. A dance that gives space to the other. So, it's done for each other, looking out for each other. A dance that gives space, you know. So, every one of us, when I say we have to die to self, part of that dying to self is to give space to others. It means leadership development, allowing others to come, going when it is your time, playing another role, whatever that means . . . to affirm, to encourage, to mentor. We are talking about radical generosity. Whatever it will take, so that God's children can participate in his eternal work.'[2]

I have told Uncle Fred's dance story numerous times, and described the powerful impact it had on me. A dance that gives space. A compelling point, expressed through a story, wrapped in culture. Timothy Tennent affirms this idea:

> We in the West have been accustomed to playing the melody. We directed the orchestra and decided what pieces would be played and where, and the players were mostly from the West. Now, the orchestra is far more diverse, and we are being asked to play harmony, not melody. This requires a temporary interlude – a time to pause and reassess, a time to think about what we are doing in fresh ways.[3]

Each one of us has a narrative or anecdote, formed by our own traditions, worldview or family values. We have ways of reading Scripture and understanding God; we have cultural strengths and weaknesses, cultural discernment and insight, cultural blind spots and biases, intuitive connection across cultures, or baggage and a history of hurt that acts as a roadblock. When we come together as a family – colourful, seasoned, mixed – we provide for one another's needs. Think of Uncle Fred's dance story, his insight and cultural wisdom, and how he points to the Trinity as an example. It is a priceless gift.

Adrian Pei, in his insightful book *The Minority Experience*, explains:

> Ultimately, diversity is about the value and dignity of people – ethnic minorities – whose unique voices have been overlooked or even silenced. It is about restoring beautiful missing pieces of the canvas of history that can enrich our view of the world, and of God . . . [It asks,] 'What perspectives and contributions are we missing?'[4]

Sharing space, giving voice, restoring missing pieces of the canvas, asking what we are forgetting, which perspectives we need to hear

– these are all important parts of the conversation as we consider the role of culture in our formation into Christlike, outward-focused people. We are all fashioned by culture, but do we recognise our blind spots, gaps and need of others in this area of shaping?

Although I have lived and taught in this intercultural space for many years, I continue to learn from and with others in this area. Several years ago, the Spirit revealed some things to me, helping me grow in fidelity and love. I have gone to the same church for many years now. It was the church that my family began going to when I returned from the Philippines just shy of 11 years of age. It was medium-sized then, with a lively youth group. Over the years it slowly dwindled with a split here, a disagreement over the constitution there, young people marrying and leaving, no significant Sunday school or youth group to draw more families. It was the church from which I left to study in the USA and to which I then returned, although to a changed version. It was the church that sent me to live and serve in South Asia, prayed and supported me, encouraged me, and to which I again returned. Over the years, the membership had shifted from mostly Anglo to beautifully multi-ethnic.

Some years ago, though, I was going through a season of discontent. I was feeling a little disconnected and at times lonely at church. I began to wonder if it was time for me to move on from this community. But it had been my faith family on and off for over thirty-five years and I was hesitant. Just as I thought I had found a new church community, Covid hit, and Australia went into lockdown. Well . . . I was not going to leave and join a new church via some video link. So, I continued with my own little church.

But several things happened in that first year of Covid. I fell in love with my small church. Our pastor and his wife led it with intention and committed friendship. I would either lead the service or preach once a month or so, which meant video-link practice on Friday nights, which in turn meant I was getting to know a small group of people better. Each Sunday, as we gathered via the video conferencing platform, someone would share their Covid story as part of the service – a personal account of losing work, or doing school online, or creating, or struggling. Even Chinese men, who are not often known to show much emotion, displayed their vulnerability. It was incredibly powerful. At the end of the service everyone was promoted as a video conference participant, and we would greet one another, celebrating one another and our sense of belonging. I learned more names. I heard more stories. I began to pray for these people, my people.

Since my pastor and his wife have come to my church, things have changed. They have brought with them characteristics enhanced by their own Chinese culture and poured it out on our church. Sharing fellowship at the end of the online service, having someone tell their story each week – I suspect those ideas emerged out of their high value for relationship. The way in which my pastor's wife reaches out, her ebullience evident, her love for others as easy to see as the smile on her face . . . It is enchanting and adds so much to our church. God has used their cultural background as they lead our community.

God used two other realisations to build my love for this group of his people. I was attending a Lausanne conference on 'diaspora', that is, dispersed peoples of the world. Time and again people would refer to the diaspora church that they attended. It was as though the Lord reached out and gently tapped me on the head. 'That is what I attend – a diaspora church,' came the realisation. It is a multicultural church, filled with people with close family in their country of origin and strong ties to their homeland. This new awareness was especially meaningful because the region of the organisation with which I serve includes an area focused on reaching diaspora peoples. The Lord used that conference to remind me: 'Yes, these are your people. I have entrusted you to them, and them to you. Live into it.'

The other revelation began through a conversation with a colleague around the Black Lives Matter protests and the broader discussion around racism. This was followed by multiple dialogues on how we can model Jesus in our organisational response at a point in time where a conversation we have been having for years has gained momentum. One aspect of this is the importance of practising holy courage by having intentional but often uncomfortable conversations. That allows us to deal with our reality rather than skirting around the edges of it. Our organisation has come a long way, but there are still many growth areas.

The idea of being uncomfortable stayed with me. For many of our non-Western brothers and sisters, coming to a conference or meeting means feeling like outsiders, sensing that they are always the ones who bend 'to accommodate the majority culture'.[5] So much is uncomfortable, awkward, other. 'Ah,' I thought. 'Until this year, that was how I often felt when going to church' – although my discomfort was a raindrop in comparison to the ocean waters within which many of my Global South friends swim. At church, even though the formal service is conducted in English, the heart conversations are often in Mandarin, surrounding me with a language I do not speak, despite my attempts to learn it through an app on my phone! Before 2021, I would not often have meaningful conversations after church that touched my heart. It was not uncommon for me to sit alone. Uncomfortable. But I have needed this experience because that 'outsider' feeling is not my norm. Usually I belong, I fit in, I network or know people. The way things are organised connects with me. That is my norm. I have needed this feeling of being other, being out of my comfort zone on a regular basis, as a point of identification with those within my organisation or sphere of engagement who I care about, believe in, and want to be in a dance with, a dance that shares space. I know that what I have experienced in the past on many a Sunday is only a shadow of what others have lived, a paltry echo of their unease or pain. Pei again reminds us that 'a key component of the minority experience [is] self-doubt'.[6] I do not experience that when I go to church on Sundays. I know I am loved and wanted, that what I have to offer when I preach or share is invited, that the linguistic shyness I feel is reflected by others who struggle with English. It is nothing like the experience many others have had, but I need this reminder, tiny though it may be. For through it, faithfulness is formed, fidelity is fashioned, love is strengthened, and within my modest church I grow comfortable with being 'other'. It is part of our mutual exchange, one to the other.

I am continuing to learn more about cultural oppression. This includes discerning the difference between personal prejudice – unveiled through negative perceptions of others, expressed in a variety of behaviours, sometimes subtle, sometimes aggressive – and institutional racism, with its imbalance of power. I am seeking to learn more about cultural bias and racial bias, about dominant and non-dominant cultures, about how I have benefited from systemic injustice. Part of this is distinguishing between what is cultural commentary and what is a call to a biblical and better way, and seeing what my part in all of this is. It is a slow and humbling journey. I do not want to automatically assume that my attitudes are righteous, that I do not offend others, even if by accident or through naivety. I want to hear the ache, the heartbreak, of my brothers and sisters with different-coloured skin who have been wronged, especially those within my sphere. I want to ask with Tracey Michae'l Lewis-Giggetts, 'What does one do when the shame is wrapped in love?'[7] What if I am the one bringing unrealised shame in the fumbled wrappings of love? How can I, too, 'believe our Creator wants more',[8] and be a part of a Christ-orientated, outward-focused people who celebrate and encourage the image of God in those around us, especially those who have been unwillingly bent into the shape of the majority culture. Hand in hand with a mosaic of fellow believers, I want to ask how we can move ahead together, in a way that honours all of those involved, particularly those who have not had the opportunity to dance in the circle yet but have been waiting for a very long time to do so. Such communal recognition and reconciliation is always costly, but it is a worthy pursuit, a multicoloured formation into the likeness of Christ for the sake of the world. After all:

> The mission belongs to God and not to us. And for the sake of his glory, he has deliberately spread the pieces of the puzzle in all the Christian cultures of the world. We cannot dismiss any culture's contribution, no matter how highly we think of our own. All the pieces of the puzzle which have been deposited within the various Christian cultural entities around the world must be brought to the table.[9]

We need one another. We reflect Jesus more clearly when we do so together.

Formation questions

1 How have you been culturally shaped (perhaps by more than one culture)?
2 What ways of thinking or cultural values do you need to release, let go of, die to?
3 What are aspects of your culture that you want to gift to others?
4 How can we celebrate one another's cultures, living out Revelation 7:9–10 now?
5 How can you affirm, encourage, make room for, mentor, practise radical generosity with those not of your own culture so that, as Uncle Fred says, they can participate in God's eternal work?
6 How can we become more like Jesus together?

10

Formed from . . . age

The accumulated wisdom of years

When I was a child growing up in the Philippines, from time to time we would visit the mountainous region of Banaue, in the northern province of Ifugao. We wound around the narrow mountain roads in a rattly old bus. The rice terraces encircled us like patchwork quilts, hues of bright grass green, golden lime, stitched together with thin pathways of packed earth. One rice paddy was layered on top of another and another, until they disappeared into the mist.

Our years are like that, building one on the other, layering one another, so to speak. Years follow months and days; experiences are intertwined with seasons. Insights are sharpened through failure; sorrow and learning are intermingled. They are all pieces woven together into a patchwork of what has formed us and of what we have to offer others.

When we consider living as outward-focused gospel people, whatever stage of life we are in, the leading up to that stage has shaped us, formed us for what is now, what is next. Each stage is valuable, necessary for God's mission in the world.

When I returned to Australia after serving among an Asian slum community for about eight years, I remember thinking, 'How do you top that?' I had worked alongside the most amazing women as together we ministered from our church hub. We loved and served the most incredible collection of women and children who woke daily to profound poverty. Over the years we were involved in a range of expressions of mission that brought life and transformation, small though it was, combining community development and gospel sharing. It seemed to me then that surely those would be my best years. 'Lord, don't let those be my best years,' I prayed.

But these present years, now, *they* are the best years, or at least the most consistently joyful, although so vastly different from my time in Southeast Asia. Those years formed me for how I am pouring myself out now, years that brought victory and heartbreak, lessons and disappointments, deep friendships and the knowledge that I still have a long way to go. The following years in my organisation's national office refined those lessons from a completely different angle. Now, there is convergence, a kind of service I unreservedly embrace. It is only because of the accumulated knowledge, hopefully coupled with wisdom, that I can embrace this latest work; the deepening reservoir of experience allows me to engage with it now in a way I could not have done back then. My hope is that every stage of life and ministry is the best yet.

When I think about the gift of age, whether it be youth, middle age or senior years, Julie comes to mind. She is one of my heroes. She had long desired to serve among Native Americans in the USA, but fullness of family life instead opened opportunities in her home nation. It was only when she retired that she could turn to new things, then reaching out to our organisation to see if we would be willing to send her into cross-cultural mission. You see, Julie was in her early seventies when she applied to live and serve missionally overseas. A lot of organisations have a policy of bringing people home at 65, so they would not consider sending someone past that age. It is crazy! Go take care of your grandkids, read, volunteer, play golf. Right? But I suppose the real question is: why not? She was in good health; she also had a deep sense of calling, a vibrant faith and a joyful heart. Who would not want her on their team? So, we sent her, at 75 years of age. Significantly, it was because of her age, her white hair, her gracious grandmotherly demeanour, that she was so readily embraced and automatically respected. She was there for about six years, with countless opportunities to speak into the lives of the Native American students she loved and served, primarily because of the status that her age gave her. Julie is a wonderful reminder that it is never too late.

There are others that I know who sour with age. They are ashamed of losing their youth, of sliding into middle age, or of reaching an age where they feel sidelined. They assert themselves with an edge rather than softness; they loom over others, seeking to retain whatever remnant of control they once had. They grasp and hold on to their pockets of influence, rather than releasing control of these areas into the hands of the next generation, trusting that they, too, can steward responsibility well. The years have shaped such people too, of course, but I wonder if, through various challenges, they have reacted rather than responded to the Spirit of God, or they have blamed God rather than genuinely sought to glorify him above all else, no matter what the cost. Such people are often respected, but they are not necessarily loved. The mark they leave on others so often steals rather than gives life. They miss the appeal and artistry found around them, seeing it through the eyes of judgement rather than acceptance. We have all known people like this. Perhaps, from time to time, we have all been someone like this.

As I age, and those coming after me seem younger and younger and yet so very sure of themselves and what they have to offer, it is easy to view youth in the same way as some critique old age, believing that people in that stage of life are somehow not enough. The apostle Paul's reminder to Timothy, his mentee, sits well here. 'Don't let anyone think less of you because you are young,' he says encouragingly (1 Timothy 4:12). His words are set within the larger context of verses 6–13:

> If you explain these things to the brothers and sisters, Timothy, you will be a worthy servant of Christ Jesus, one who is nourished by the message of faith and the good teaching

you have followed. Do not waste time arguing over godless ideas and old wives' tales. Instead, train yourself to be godly. 'Physical training is good, but training for godliness is much better, promising benefits in this life and in the life to come.' This is a trustworthy saying, and everyone should accept it. This is why we work hard and continue to struggle, for our hope is in the living God, who is the Savior of all people and particularly of all believers.

Teach these things and insist that everyone learn them. Don't let anyone think less of you because you are young. Be an example to all believers in what you say, in the way you live, in your love, your faith, and your purity. Until I get there, focus on reading the Scriptures to the church, encouraging the believers, and teaching them.

Timothy, formed through his own family heritage mentioned in 2 Timothy 1:5, and through the influence of his mentor, Paul, is urged to continue the process of formation, training himself 'to be godly'. He in turn influences others from a place of spiritual maturity, despite his youth. He is to model godliness through word, life witness and character, bringing the truth of Scripture alive to those turning to 'godless ideas and old wives' tales'. He is young in years but mature in faith, both in the choices he makes and in the model he sets for other people.

K. John Amalraj, in a chapter titled 'What Shapes Our Spirituality in Missions?', considers the changing tides of life-stages.[1] Young people often eagerly embrace the many and varied prospects that come their way. Activity is welcomed. Busyness is valued. But age often reshapes how we choose to spend our time and energy. We are more discerning about what we engage in. We seek to invest in others coming behind us. We take the long view. Amalraj reminds us, though, that we need a generational mix partnering together for God's mission in the world. Otherwise, there is imbalance, narrow perspectives and an absence of mutuality. Although Amalraj is writing with a focus on expressions of spirituality rather than the tool that age or life stage can be in the formation process, his reminder of the 'need for intergenerational participation at every level of mission work' is timely.[2] One generation brings energy, insight into technological language, the ability to exegete the contemporary culture. Another generation brings long sight over a vast horizon of time, a deep well of knowledge, learning, lessons, experience and change. Others fall somewhere in between. Each expression is needed. They are all teachers if we have the posture to learn.

My niece is in her early twenties. She has a passion for adventure, keeping a kayak, stand-up paddle board and underwater camera within easy reach. Some time ago we spent the afternoon on her SUP, which rolled into a walk along the esplanade, her recycled fold-up hammock in hand. We found a spot under the pier and hung up the hammock to watch the sun go down, chatting as we swung. 'Do you ever do anything alone?' I asked, being someone who would feel very comfortable going for a solo kayak trip. 'No, not really,' she replied. 'I always find a friend to explore with.' And she told me of rowing with this person or hiking to hang the hammock with that person. She always takes someone with her. It is her way of building authentic relationship and investing in her people.

As I thought about it later, a recent sermon I had preached about the encounter with the risen Christ on the road to Emmaus came to mind (Luke 24:13–35). Jesus came alongside the two believers, walking with them in comfortable conversation, explaining and revealing truths as he went along. It was discipleship in motion. That is what my niece is good at: coming alongside, spending time together with others in organic, communal discipleship, living and speaking out Jesus amid the everyday.

I witnessed it again on the final morning of her bridal shower. A group of Jesus-loving women had gathered, most of them her friends from church or university days. They spoke of my niece's impact on them, her pursuit and encouragement and relational investment in them, of her passion for books of the Bible. At the end, they all pulled out their phones. They had decided to read the Bible together – all the Gen Z-ers in the room. They all had the app downloaded, and one by one they took turns where they sat, each reading out a portion of Scripture. Young woman after young woman after young woman . . . every single one of them. They were in this together, an online community committed to reading God's word together. They were doing discipleship their way, through their generational lens. It would be easy to say that discipleship was centred on technology for these digital natives, but that was not the case. It was centred on Jesus. It was enabled by technology. It was Jesus-centred, outward-focused living, Gen Z style.

Formation questions

1 How has God used the various stages of your life to shape you, to shape the next stage?

2 When you move into a new season, are you able to let go and release control to others? Are you harbouring something that is holding you back?

3 Are you seeking to be mature in Christ, no matter how many or how few years you have spent on earth?

4 How are you ensuring that this season of your life and ministry is the best yet?

5 How are you coming alongside others, discipling them amid everyday life, as Jesus did?

6 Are you investing in those around you, raising up the next generation? If so, how?

11

Formed from . . . gender: women

The opportunities and barriers our gender brings (part I)

We are formed from gender: 'male and female he created them' (Genesis 1:27), and whether male or female, we are shaped by being one or the other. This can have an impact on our chosen roles or those withheld from us, the opportunities provided, or the doors closed. It may influence how we spend our time, what our priorities are, or the questions we ask in order to understand the world. This might be because of cultural expectations (national, organisational or church culture) around gender identity, despite the non-binary conversation happening today. The list goes on. We are formed from gender. Interestingly, as I discussed this concept with a range of colleagues and friends, only the women had considered the impact of their gender on their formation process. Almost all the men I talked to had not previously turned this idea over. They metaphorically sat back with a loud exhalation. 'Aah . . . that's an interesting question. I've never thought of that before', or some variation of those words. Perhaps that contrast itself says a lot, because many women I have spoken to about this topic are acutely aware of gender matters as they are shaped by the Spirit into gospel people.

As a woman, when I consider the astounding women who have influenced me, I am in awe. My mother is primary among these, someone who loved and discipled me with prayerful intention. An adopted aunt who modelled living a full life as a single person is significant. The list continues with prayer partners and close friends who have accepted me without reservation and loved me fully despite my quirks. These are women who have pointed me to Jesus time and time again. There is something precious about being a part of the worldwide sisterhood, a sacred space of commonality despite other areas of divergence. For those men reading these words, I am sure the women who have influenced your lives leap to mind – mothers and wives, sisters and teachers. The same is true for influential men in our lives.

As someone without male siblings, I am grateful for the trusted men who have become my brothers, spread around the world. They grant a perspective other than my own. I am thankful for the sisters with whom I have journeyed, whether it be women I have received from, ministered to or travelled alongside – kindred spirits, heart friends, sisters beyond blood. Being a woman has opened unique, privileged opportunities that I would not have had as a man. I would never have sat on the floor among a group of slum women, leaning against one another, elbows and arms draped on knees, deeply immersed in conversation, bound by a sisterhood. If I were a man, I might not have been attuned to hearing my own mother's story in the same way. I probably would not have been entrusted with heart stories from wounded women quite so quickly, if ever. Doors have been opened into the lives of others because I am a woman.

Of course, the reverse is also true. Growing up in the global mission world, choosing to study theology and to serve in mission as an adult has brought me rich and wonderful experiences, but it is often a man's world. This is especially as it relates to leadership. In many a missional leadership meeting, I am either the only woman or one of a few women. The men are my brothers. I do not resent the situation, but it has been challenging at times. I am not the only woman who shares this lived reality.

On reading a book foreword that Mark Labberton had written, I found myself responding with surprising emotion. Explaining about his shared background with his brother, he admitted that being born male 'spared us many residual sexualist limitations and opened doors that undoubtedly made some things much easier for us than for girls of our ages'.[1] 'Oh yes,' that resonates, I thought as I read. 'Thank you for acknowledging that.'

Thinking about the dual opportunities and barriers that have arisen from being female, I look back at the slow shift to include women in our organisational leadership structure. A female Team Leader was appointed here, an Area Leader there. Husband and wife co-appointments became normal over time. Several women were intentionally invited on to one of the organisational leadership bodies as part of the rotating practice to represent the 'Ground Zero' of our organisation. In the last several years, a woman has been entrusted with one of our most senior field leadership roles in her own right. Opportunities have gradually been extended. However, in the organisational background consistent barriers have loomed, like the hurdles in a race, some of them easily spotted, some arising suddenly, causing shock and disorientation.

Personally, one of those times was when a think tank was being held around a topic that was tucked into my area of responsibility and sphere of influence. When my local leadership was asked who to send to represent my missional community, someone else was chosen because of the opportunity it presented to him. There was no thought given to the fact that, as a woman, I too would have found this to be an incredible opportunity, especially since the focus lay within my area of contribution. When the initial flare of hurt dimmed, I felt deep disappointment. I walked away feeling overlooked and diminished. Honestly, I think it was an unintentional slight, but it left me feeling as though all that I poured out in my area of responsibility was not seen, not valued, not worthy – to such a degree that I was not even considered for this professional development opportunity to wrestle robustly with an important topic within a broader sphere. It was a profoundly demotivating experience.

These matters are complex and rarely about just one thing, but they have an impact on our formation. Was the above issue a matter of gender? Not entirely. Was it to do with personality on both sides, or another agenda at hand? Probably, at least partially. Was it because of the established systems that were the reality at at the time, systems based on inherent assumptions around male leadership, defaulting to these leaders providing opportunities for those made in their likeness? Perhaps.

Dominique DuBois Gilliard provides a contrast. Noting that he cannot abandon his maleness, he explains that he can use the related privilege

> when I am in relationships of accountability with my sisters. I can discern with them how I go about leveraging my influence, platform, and voice to advocate for [them]. I can learn from my sisters how I can advocate on their behalf in helpful ways . . . I can recommend my sister anytime I get asked for recommendations . . . I can investigate why so few sisters are at tables of power; use my platform to uplift how Scripture calls us to affirm, see, and treat women . . . I can also humbly and publicly confess when I get it wrong and commit to doing and being better without making excuses.[2]

Gilliard further explains the need for greater investment in women of colour, for whom there is often a double stacking-against. They 'are constantly overlooked for leadership development and mentoring opportunities'.[3] Part of my formation may include being a woman, with related opportunities and barriers, but I still hold on to the benefits and privileges of being a white woman.

Another story comes to mind, one shared with permission.

Many years ago, the Lord made it clear that it was time for me to step away from involvement with one mission-related team and turn to something new. What would it be? The person I reported to was overseeing three times the normal number of teams, and was often ill, tired and unresponsive to emails. I wondered if he needed help. I had assisted the former person in this role and thought that perhaps there was an opportunity to stay in the nation I had come to love but to use a different part of my gift-mix. When I shyly approached him, he nicely backed away. 'No, there is nothing you can contribute at this time.' Years later he admitted that he did not invite me on to his team when there was obvious need because he felt threatened.

Although I do not live with regret or resentment (that is no way to live!), I admit I would have really loved the opportunity to minister within a broader area than at the team level I had been serving at. I would have loved to mix pastoral and strategic gifting in a new way, within a different context, among a diverse set of people. Others within the area had asked if I was interested in serving in that way, so there seemed to be an openness to my involvement. But . . . no. The invitation was not extended. It was a confusing time. It involved much grief: grief for my lost hope of serving in another way; grief over leaving a country and people I loved; grief over moving back to my home country, which, as a third-culture kid, is home but not home; grief in thinking that for some reason I was not quite enough. Because that was my assumption – that I had not been invited to join his team because something was wrong with me. At the time it was painful, and it saddens me to think of the doors he closed to others in those earlier years because of his own personal struggle.

Another role opened up for me outside Asia, a role which allowed me to serve and grow as a leader, as a teacher, as a creative initiator. It brought me to a conference where, years on from this initial closed door, I found myself sitting at a table with this man and his wife. They are precious friends, friends I have laughed and cried with, played and ministered with, and people who have been on their own vast journey of healing and growth, awareness and empowerment. I am not sure how this matter arose, but he laughed and said: 'I don't know why we didn't ask you on to our team then. We are asking you to consider it now. Will you?' 'Oh . . . ah . . .' I stuttered in surprise. I took a big breath. Should I be vulnerable? 'Is truth-telling here worth it?' I asked myself silently. 'Is it helpful rather than hurtful?' It was at that table, amid the noise of surrounding conversations and the clatter of cutlery, that I first shared about the grief that took place in my heart when I was leaving our nation of service all those years ago. That was the moment when this brother first reflected on why an invitation had not been extended. Because of the healing that had taken place, he could now admit that he had felt threatened, that the absence of invitation expressed a protective stance rather than an act of discernment. Together, as sacred siblings, we were emerging from the shadow that lies over hurt secreted away and left unspoken.

Nevertheless, I was hesitant. The shadow was lighter, but it still lingered. I could not completely believe that if I now accepted this couple's offer, this brother would celebrate my contribution, freeing me into it. Could I practise my teaching gifts? Would he interpret my desire to initiate and fully own my responsibilities as strong or aggressive behaviour, an approach which in men is more often termed 'being assertive' and 'displaying initiative'? After days and days of prayer and reflection, I wrote a long email, sharing my thoughts, my heart. I waited for a response. One week passed. Two weeks. A month. My email was never answered, and trust was frayed, confirming that I had been right to hesitate. When I asked him about this lack of response some time later, he said that he did not know how to respond, and so he left it. Again, I was left with the vague feeling that I had done something wrong, that I was not enough. I was just not sure how.

The story continues. For me to share this narrative of my own shaping by the Spirit with you as readers, it was only right to reach out to this dear friend for perspective to present a fuller picture and permission to share his brokenness. I was nervous – really nervous. How would he react? He and his wife had responded with grace at the table all those years ago. Over the decades their acts of building trust outweighed their acts of breaking trust. I could trust them in this. Gathering holy courage, I reached out, and he replied warmly. He asked to have a video call so that he, his wife and I could talk together. Over several hours I shared and they listened. He modelled a powerful and consistent humility, asking for forgiveness, affirming the importance of wrestling with this topic of gender.

During our time together, I listened too. I heard of their dual journey, of the Spirit's shaping work, how they have found healing and engaged in learning which has freed them from certain understandings of what marriage or missional community or male and female dynamics should be. Because of my old leader's own formation journey, he now consciously and actively looks for ways to open the door for those with less opportunity, especially for those for whom the door is stuck. They now echo my present leader – a leader with whom I feel, as a woman, wholeheartedly welcome in the missional leadership space. It is a rare experience.

Situations like this can break trust, or we can choose to trust another more consistent, faithful one: God revealed in Jesus. His outcomes for our lives are good, no matter what is given or what is withdrawn.

Several years ago, my organisation invited Mary Lederleitner, author of the insightful book *Women in God's Mission: Accepting the invitation to serve and lead*, to speak at a webinar within which she asked the question 'How has gender impacted your personal leadership development process?' That is a more focused topic than the one we are exploring, but we could adapt the question to 'How has your gender been part of how the Spirit has shaped you? How has gender had an impact on your own formation into a gospel-centred, outward-focused person?'

It has shaped the *what*. The focus and purpose of participating in God's mission in the world is often defined by the context in which a person or family is engaging. What is acceptable in this place, with those people? Can men and women interact platonically as sacred siblings in that environment or does that break cultural taboos?

It has probably shaped the *when*, since many women invest in their homes and children for a season, while their spouses participate in broader opportunities. This can cause the corresponding but disparate emotions of fulfilment *and* frustration, as with many gifted female friends I have known over the years. They have watched their respective husbands' paths open up and wondered if it is OK to long for missional opportunities themselves, and yet they are exhausted at every turn because of a household of lively children. They are mostly satisfied, while still feeling the small itch of holy discontent.

It may have shaped the *why*. Leaders can be slow to recognise what a woman can give because she has less chance than a man to participate in public ministry. Consequently, women are overlooked when an invitation is extended for someone to take up one role or another. Or perhaps some leaders quietly think that a woman should not hold such a position, regardless of the official stance of an organisation or church.

It will have shaped the *how*. As women practise transformational leadership more regularly, they often opt to use terms such as 'facilitator' rather than 'leader', since these intuitively make others, men and women alike, more comfortable. Additionally, women will at times ask different questions from those that men ask, because they frequently frame the world in a different way.

It may be helpful to explore some attributes of missional women and how this has an impact on their experience. Lederleitner describes seven characteristics that women of influence in mission regularly display as they desire to be both faithful and connected.

Such women discern the need for a threefold anchoring: 'to their God, to the people they meet through their ministries, and to the realities present within their ministry contexts'.[4] The seven traits include giving up power, prioritising intimate communion with the Lord, and preferring collaborative leadership. Additionally, they involve seeing value in holistic mission, having a sensitivity towards injustice (including but broader than gender discrimination), and caring for relational disharmony in personal ministry situations. Finally, these female leaders reflect an intentionality towards lifelong learning as they serve with excellence.

Research has also shown that there is a gender gap regarding confidence. 'A study done at Cornell University found that men overestimate their abilities and performance, while women underestimate both. In fact, their actual performance does not differ in quality or quantity.'[5] Although this finding is within a business setting, the principle remains.

The above study reminds me of a beloved colleague who was a joy to work with, but oh, I saw this confidence lived out in him. He is a gifted, vibrant person, who would put his hand up for this and that opportunity, regardless of his knowledge level or skill. His thought was, 'Well, I can learn and develop in time for that presentation or prospect.' By contrast, a woman will generally wait until she has gained the knowledge or skill before volunteering for the same opening. Nancy Clark cites a Hewlett-Packard (HP) survey in which

> [w]omen working at HP applied for a promotion only when they believed they met 100 percent of the qualifications listed for the job. Men were happy to apply when they thought they could meet 60 percent of the job requirements.

Clark writes: 'Men are confident about their ability at 60%, but women don't feel confident until they've checked off each item on the list. Think about the difference between 60% and 100%.'[6] Again, the focus is business-related, but nonetheless, a hidden truth emerges: women will often require additional encouragement and opportunity to say yes to an invitation or opening.

It is an interesting thought that we are formed through our experience of gender. We are entrusted with the richness and wonder of our gender, the barriers and challenges of our gender. We hold the opportunities of our gender, the heartbreak and struggles of our gender, the expectations of country or church or organisational culture related to our gender. We can rejoice with thanks or shake our fists at the injustice we have experienced, real or perceived, intended or not. Or we can recognise what has been, accept the part it has played in our formation process, and bring important and healthy change to our own sphere of influence with grace-filled intention and commitment. We can do this by being thoughtful, by opening doors for those who regularly meet barriers, by intentionally nurturing minorities in the missional leadership space and by honouring one another as sacred siblings. We can also do this by having the courage to hold uncomfortable conversations, building awareness with our male leaders, who may often do something out of thoughtlessness rather than malice and simply need to be reminded that there is another perspective. Sometimes, though, this courage will mean combining grace and strength to say: 'That is not right. That is an expression of gender bias. Please make room in the circle for this woman with something to give.'

Meanwhile, we can trust that God is at work in our daily Christ-witness in profound, privileged and celebrated ways because of our gender as women.

Formation questions

1 How has the Spirit used your gender as a woman to form you?

2 Who are the women who have been a shaping influence in your life?

3 What are you truly grateful for having experienced simply because you were born female?

4 What limitations, walls or hurts have you experienced because you are a woman?

5 How can you grow in courage, believing that you or women you lead have something meaningful to offer?

6 How can you advocate on behalf of other women who are quietly waiting for doors to open to them so they can be involved more broadly in God's mission in the world?

12

Formed from . . . gender: men

The opportunities and barriers our gender brings (part 2)

The previous chapter was reflecting on the experience of women, a group who seem to be more aware of the role of gender in formation, probably highlighted by the consistent barriers they encounter. What about the men? How does gender have an impact on their formation process?

As an unmarried woman without brothers, I reached out to a handful of my male friends, asking them how being male has influenced their formation for mission. As I mentioned before, it was a new thought for most of them, but I am so grateful for sacred siblings who are self-aware, reflective and willing to share vulnerably about their own journey.

Here is what I asked these men:

- How has being male / a man formed you for mission?
- (Or a variation) How has being a guy had an impact on your formation journey?
- What opportunities has your maleness provided?
- What barriers or challenges has your maleness presented?
- Finally, today, what does it mean for you, as a man, to continue being made into the image of Christ for the sake of others?

Their responses were quite varied, even for a small selection of men from four nations, who have lived in and been influenced by seven cultures outside their home country.

When considering how being male has formed them as outward-focused men of Jesus, several spoke of their testosterone-driven desire for action and adventure, where they move towards risk while wanting to protect those they love. They are motivated towards significance, roles where they can make a difference in the world, with a deep, almost aggressive ambition towards initiating something, towards activity and achievement, change, a vision for more. This ties in with the idea of leaving a legacy. Anecdotal though this may be, in my experience the idea of legacy almost always comes from a man. Men want to leave their mark on the world and be remembered. Of course, it is not only men who want this, but perhaps the pattern exists more consistently within a male set than across both genders.

When asked how being a man has had an impact on their formation journey, my colleagues and friends noted the influence that male mentors, stereotypes and cultural expectations have exerted on their lives. For one man, there was the expectation to lead. Another brother talked about the push to make a name for himself, to expand his own kingdom. A good gift from God – being entrusted to extend God's kingdom rule – can be twisted and turned to our own purposes. His formation journey has included constant surrender: surrender of the assumption that he can do something in his own strength; surrendering the default position of trusting in his own wisdom and instincts above the understanding of God; surrendering the habit of racing ahead of God rather than learning to walk in relationship with him, something he notices his wife finds more natural.

Several of these brothers touched on the struggle of many men around moral purity, and the zigzag pathway of formation this includes, with shades of darkness and redemption mixed together. I wonder if it would be helpful to visit the idea of *sacred sibling* here, a term I have used a couple of times over these pages on gender. The reason is that it seems the wrestle with moral purity can often act as a barrier to forming healthy relationships across genders within the family of God as we bear witness in this world.

Lederleitner describes how the term 'sacred sibling' captured her 'imagination as a healthy metaphor for the mission workplace'.[1] She goes on:

> I love this term because it presents a vision that can help us imagine new ways of working together without explicitly or implicitly sending messages to women that they are temptresses or stumbling blocks . . . I have four brothers, and though my friends might have thought they were handsome or were attracted to them, I never saw my brothers that way. They were just my brothers. And even among those who are married, the percentage of the time spent in sexual activity is quite small.
>
> If sexual activity comprises only a small part of marriage, why are we allowing concerns about sex to overshadow our work environments? Shouldn't we create structures that will reveal to the world the beauty of God's sons and daughters as they grow together in Christlikeness?[2]

So often, because of the tug and pull towards impure thoughts and actions, a separation is created, dividing gospel-focused men and women, and preventing them from having holy and healthy familial relationships – being sacred siblings. Because of that, women can be sidelined, with doors of opportunities closed to them because of the fears of some of their male colleagues. Because some men do not trust opening their hearts and minds to a woman who is not their wife or sister, they shut off the possibility of having a life-giving, God-honouring relationship with their sister in the Lord. Will men need to be wise in this interaction? Of course. As the authors of *Mixed Ministry* write:

Picture a married couple facing each other, gazing into each other's eyes. This depth of intimacy is inappropriate for siblings. Instead picture a brother and sister facing forward, gazing off into the distance in the same direction. They stand side by side, focusing on a mutual goal. For sacred siblings, that goal is ministry, honoring God, and furthering his kingdom. Again, the emotional attachment of a wife versus that of a sister is different.

Knowing the difference is crucial, and siblings who are careless or foolish destroy lives and the Lord's reputation. What would Jesus applaud as appropriate for siblings?[3]

This fear of trusting themselves with women, and thus sidelining them, will not be true for all men, of course, and it is perhaps exacerbated in some cultures more than others. As an Australian, I find this behaviour much more common in some of my American male colleagues from a particular church background. My guess is, though, that this attitude resonates with some readers. However, in the midst of these temptations, how do we keep asking: 'How can I bring out the best aspects of my sisters and brothers in Christ in appropriate and God-honouring ways? How can we be formed into Christ-honouring, outward-focused people as sacred siblings?'

But it is more than that. The account in Genesis 1 – 3 sees the creation of both a man and a woman. Although theology may differ on the hierarchy or equality of this order, there is no doubt that the two were created to live and work together as co-rulers. Just as we are less without other cultures, man is less without woman, and woman is less without man. We need each other – in church life and outward-focused witness. Our contribution is better together. We reflect God more wholly together. Our enemy loves division, situations where only one set is represented, whether culture or gender. Part of our subversive witness is to say: 'We choose dual representation. We choose co-rulership. We choose to bear witness as sacred siblings.' This pushes back the kingdom of darkness and welcomes the kingdom of light. Then we can ask, to paraphrase Lederleitner, 'How can we reveal to the world the beauty of God's sons and daughters as we grow together in Christlikeness?'

Returning to the questions listed above, for all of the men I questioned, the opportunities they encountered were multiple. Doors were opened, chances provided. They were encouraged to lead and urged to engage others in Christ-conversations. One man responded with an inner-life example, where the opportunity lies in the

> drive to be a part of God's kingdom in a meaningful way, to be making forward progress in the pilgrimage of becoming more like Jesus. The epic nature of this adventure is something I find deeply compelling . . . to be a part of something much bigger than myself and to play an important role in that.

To him, this is God's great opportunity. Although these words may resonate with many women as well, I wonder if the confidence to pursue such a desire and the doors opened along the way reflects the male formation journey more than the female. Perhaps this is worth considering.

One Brazilian man reflected that being a man allowed for more freedom to stay out late or sleep over at the home of a mentor or church leader. This was an opportunity not presented to the women of his culture. Yet it provided time for deeper relationship, for holistic life-on-life mentoring, for observation and conversation, which was essential for his formation, especially his shaping as a leader.

It was fascinating to hear of the various barriers and challenges each of these men pinpointed, or the lack thereof. Several admitted that they had not faced many, which one discerned as being a probable hallmark of a man in church or missional leadership. This same man had certainly not experienced what he knows some of his female colleagues have experienced.

When my male friends went on to identify barriers, most of these barriers were internal: temptations towards pride, self-reliance, focusing on *doing* over a blend of *being* and doing; the temptation to use and manipulate others as a means to their own end, to build their own kingdom, to achieve self-fulfilment and meet their own needs in ungodly ways. All of these are barriers to becoming more like Christ and participating fully in his mission in the world. They are obstacles mostly presented by self or sin, not by external forces, as is so often the case with women. The exception in this regard was a man who is an eldest son, a role which brings with it certain cultural expectations of care and presence in the birth family. For someone living a Christ-life outside his home country, he carries with him the guilt of his parents' unfulfilled hopes. Although it did not stop him, it has added a heavy weight to his missional journey.

One experienced colleague pointed out that, among the younger generation of men, being male is often viewed in a negative light, or at least the version of being male that they are being presented with. This younger generation sees that old stereotypes need to be dulled or perhaps even feminised. Does this lead to a diminishing of that adventurous, protecting spirit that desires to make a difference in the world? Or is it a move towards reflecting the nature of God more fully? How does this new understanding of gender form them as gospel-orientated, outward-focused people?

This is an interesting discussion – one we can only touch on in these pages. It does point to the continual inner wrestle of one of my brother's experiences. For him and many other men, there is the coaxing pull from the media or surrounding culture to be a certain kind of man. His desire is to be different from the expectations of society. He wants to love like Jesus, to listen well, to be comfortable as the tears pool into puddles in his eyes and slip down his cheeks. It is true that many '[m]en are trained to repress emotions; they are limited by the straitjacket of masculinity'.[4] Each of these examples of love, listening and crying is contrary to the male macho image often encouraged within certain cultural contexts, but they are all aspects of the person God has called my friend to be. His formation journey has included embracing expressions of emotion.

Still another dear brother vulnerably echoes this, sharing how part of his formation has been to redefine what it means to be a man. He grew up in an era and environment where sport was idolised. This was not an area of strength for him and led to a sense of humiliation. He was comfortable with emotions, with expressing himself, and was therefore drawn to friendships with women. He writes:

> Because of the cultural values placed on gender, I have struggled most of my life, wondering how I measure up as a man. I'm sure that has played into my insecurities and fear in allowing others to walk . . . more closely with me.

He goes on to note how this influenced his theology, his marriage, his leadership. He insightfully adds:

> My theological and cultural background said that men were supposed to lead – in the home and in the church. This teaching has brought so much pressure and so much dysfunction into so many marriages and leadership situations. Many men realise they really don't have what it takes or are not gifted to lead, but they feel the pressure to do so anyway . . . Being a 'man' and a 'leader' for many means that they have to be 'enough' by themselves.

It has taken years for this brother to find freedom from these cultural expectations, both the country culture and the church culture. He does not shrink from his responsibilities, but he can now embrace them from a place of redemption and freedom, rather than weighted expectation. He recognises the privileges and opportunities handed to him as a man because of the cultural tradition that he emerged from. Now he is asking: 'What would kingdom culture say? How do we factor in the Spirit's gifts?'

We are formed through gender. It is one of the many tools that God uses to shape us into his likeness. I wonder if these few pages will begin a formation journey for those male readers who have not considered this idea until now. I hope so!

Let me leave you with the final question I asked this group of brothers: 'Today, what does it mean for you, as a man, to continue being made into the image of Christ for the sake of others?' For some, your gender will distinctly mark your response. For others, less so. Either way, may the answer come from a place of self-awareness and intention as you continue pressing into mission formation for the sake of those who are yet to meet Jesus.

Formation questions

1 How have you been formed by your gender as a man?
2 Identify cultural stereotypes or expectations for your male gender. How much do you conform to these, or how, if necessary, have you sought to break from them?
3 How has your theology shaped your understanding and experience of entering into God's mission as a man?
4 Consider the opportunities that have been opened to you because of your maleness. Alternatively, what about the barriers you have experienced, the doors shut to you?
5 How have the opportunities and barriers you have experienced as a man deepened or shaken your trust of the Spirit at work in your life? What do you need to surrender to him?
6 What change do you need to seek within your sphere of influence?

13

Formed from . . . team

Influenced by our church or missional community

'Team life can be one of the greatest gifts within our mission life and service, but it can also break your heart.' After articulating this sentence years ago, I have spoken variations of it multiple times in multiple settings, preparing people as they leap into cross-cultural gospel witness. It is not necessarily original, but it is true: in both a mission context and church life, team or community forms us. It provides purpose and belonging, invites us into a supernatural synergy, and empowers us to fully step into God's grace-gifts within that context. It forms us into the likeness of Christ as we bump up against one another's personalities and cultures and quirks and foibles. It reminds us of the biblical call to interdependence above independence. It provides continuity for current ministry and nurtures fellowship, trust, accountability and longevity. When it is done well, it is life-giving. When our rights overshadow our desire to glorify God, or our brokenness rises to the surface, trust is ruptured. If not protected, team or community life can fall apart; wounds can appear, growing septic if not attended to. Yet, through the forming breath of the Holy Spirit, 'every relationship has the potential of becoming the place of transforming encounter with God'.[1] I wonder: how has this been true for you?

We are strongly shaped by those we serve with in our outward-focused, missional communities. This allows us to become 'mature in Christ in a community, not a crowd'.[2] We grow up among the collection of people we belong to with commitment and intentionality, rather than a constellation of individuals. As one of my past lecturers articulates:

The best testimony to the truth of the gospel is the quality of our life together. Jesus risked his reputation and credibility of his story by tying them to how his followers live and care for one another in community (John 17:20–23) . . . The beauty of loving communities does not replace the importance of the verbal proclamation of the gospel, but Jesus explicitly linked the truth of his life and message to our life together.[3]

Does anyone come to mind when you reflect on how Jesus links the truth of his life with the message of your life within your church community or team?

When I consider those I have served alongside, I am overwhelmed by the depth of character found in these sacred siblings. There are several teams in particular that have been a profound joy to work with as we lived out Jesus. These communities have formed me, allowing me to 'flourish and become most fully human',[4] as Christine Pohl writes, capturing the potential of the communal transformative process. Let me tell you about two of those missional teams.

The team I was a part of while living in Asia had such a profound impact on me that, although I have been gone for many years now, it continues to shape me. Nirmala, a doctor from the northeastern part of the country, led us with grace, integrity and faithfulness. Early in our time together, I sensed that I was doing things that offended her, but since my cultural insight was still developing, I could not work it out. So, I called her. 'Nirmala,' I started, 'I was wondering, when this . . . happened today, did I do something to hurt you?' 'Oh no,' she replied, laughing it off, 'it's fine.' But still, I wondered. It took my asking several more times, after more incidents, small rubs throughout our workday, before she admitted that I had indeed done this or that. She was my gracious, gentle cultural teacher. We would meet at the church and go into the slum together. Kids and women would gather around her, seeking medical advice. Patiently, she would listen and care for each of them. In Nirmala, I witnessed Christ at work.

Or Pamela, an older woman, who remains one of the most compassionate people I have ever met. She poured out the compassion of Jesus, being generous, thoughtful and sharply sensitive to the need of others. In Pamela, I witnessed Christ at work.

Or Shuba, who had the ability to share the gospel or a life-lesson with contextual insight. She never diluted the truth of her message but simplified it for the uneducated women in the slum or for the youth, for Muslim and Hindu alike. She was a woman who could have done anything, but she chose to invest her life this way. In Shuba, I witnessed Christ at work.

Or Somyia, a refugee from Central Asia who brought jewellery-making artistry to the team. Speaking multiple languages already, she picked up Hindi and Urdu along the way. She wholeheartedly poured herself into these slum women, transferring skills and belief in them, that they were worthy, precious, clever. In Somyia, I witnessed Christ at work.

Others came and went from our team, but these four were the core of the group. When one of us was missing, we felt it, because we each brought something different, necessary, valued. We knew without a doubt that we needed one another, not just to get the job done but also because we were better together, a more complete witness. I learned more about Jesus through each one of them, and they left me wanting him more.

Who has had this kind of impact on you, leaving you wanting more of Jesus?

The Regional Leadership Team (RLT) I now work with is another great joy. Truly, they blow me away and continue to form me into the likeness of Christ as we interact, discuss, challenge and enjoy one another. Over time, our Regional Leader has carefully and thoughtfully pulled together a range of people to collaboratively work, serve, enjoy fellowship, decide and lead as people joined together in God's mission in the world. It is a group consisting of the Regional Leader, multiple Area Leaders, a couple who are spearheading a mobilisation effort, another wise consultant, and me, serving in leadership development and mission formation. There are several elements at play when considering why leading in this specific missional community is so enjoyable. They may not be unique, but they work well in our context.

Within our team, we celebrate shared communication, enjoying its dynamic and engaging nature. We use a social media group as the hub of our communication. Through it we keep one another up to date with what is going on, share prayer requests, laugh at fishing photos, hear of ministry successes and challenges, upload documents for feedback, set agendas, exchange links, are vulnerable, grieve with one another and enjoy a sense of communal formation. This shared communication, then, spills over into the times when we can meet face to face, building a solid foundation of trust and interdependence.

Our commitment to one another and the communal expression of our leadership shapes our communal prayer times when, each Monday morning from 6:30 to 7 a.m., we gather online to bring our region before the Father, under a weekly rotating leadership. This allows us to journey together prayerfully, lifting one another before the Lord as a community. It also does something else. It is as though the effects of these thirty minutes of prayer seep into every level of our RLT community, deepening the foundation of *koinonia*, that Spirit-given fellowship that strengthens and encourages and spurs us on. It fills us up so that we can collectively spill out to others. Often our prayer time is wrapped around the word of God, with his truth acting as a springboard for the prayer and worship that we carry through the week until meeting again. Just as we are formed for joining in God's mission in the world through prayer as individuals, so too we have found that we continue to be formed for this same engagement as a gospel-orientated community through communal worship, enriched by time in the word and sealed with prayer. Have you ever known someone who has drawn you into prayer like that, gently inviting you to encounter Jesus more regularly?

It is mostly common practice for us to seek input from one another as an RLT. This shared input is not taken for granted but valued. Although each of us owns the responsibility of our area of influence, our Regional Leader set the tone for this early on, posturing himself in a way that invited the voices of others into the vision for the region, ideas he was wrestling with, and so on. He intuitively understood that those who help to shape and create something have a deeper ownership of it. His posture has filtered down. We value the insight voiced by trusted individuals who do not directly share our own area of responsibility and yet desire that we succeed in what has been entrusted to us. Can you relate to that sense of feeling valued, your voice listened to?

I think of my own sphere of responsibility, which includes our leadership development process, involving three week-long residential courses over a two-year timeframe, with learning tasks to be completed in between those periods of time. For the week of leadership development which we have most recently held, almost every member of my team shaped, confirmed, reformed or contributed to the time in one way or another. I would bounce ideas or content off them. They would speak into the preparation with wisdom and freedom. Many of them were facilitators during the week itself, investing themselves with vulnerability and spiritual insight. The result was much more meaningful and creative because we had worked on it together. Who comes to mind when you think, 'That person makes my life/work/ministry/ community better'?

Shared input can, but does not necessarily, lead to shared discernment and, in turn, shared decision-making. In this case, more often than not, it has done so. We are collectively aware that we all bring certain strengths and weaknesses to the table, while others on the team come with additional, enhancing gifts, as well as their own set of weaknesses. One team member has deep gifts of discernment, another prophetic gifting, still another acute business acumen and helpful impartiality. Together, through a Spirit-led sense of communal discernment, we can move ahead with decisions that we all own because we have jointly arrived at these same conclusions. Does it mean that we never make our own decisions? Of course not. There are times when we need to submit, one to the other. In humility, we witness a mutual submission in the decision-making process among this collection of leaders. This has profoundly shaped us all. Can you remember a time when you easily bent to another because they easily bent towards you?

To a degree that I find uncommon and Jesus-like, our Regional Leader has established a culture of shared power. This is a core part of living and leading in a community committed to God's mission in the world. He consistently and willingly gives up power in the form of opportunities, time, resources, ideas, advocating for others, and serving in a way that helps others succeed. 'I've been invited to a conference, but it makes more sense for you to go. Are you interested?' he has asked. Such behaviour is rare in my experience. With this model, he sets the tone for others. Following a servant-leader who is open-handed stirs in the hearts and minds of his or her followers the desire to be like that as well, because it has the fragrance of Christ. There are echoes of this kind of posture and thinking throughout our mission region, as we talk about giving up self for the sake of *koinonia* within a multicultural context. Who do you know who practises this uncommon sharing of power?

Having such a rich and meaningful experience of gospel-centred community is life-giving. Have we messed up? Absolutely. Still, we are quick to overlook mistakes, to reach out to and reconcile with our colleagues, having those uncomfortable conversations that lead to clarification and forgiveness. We listen, bending our ears to one another. We learn, chewing on questions asked from an angle different from our norm. We continue to be formed by those we serve with, our community given to seeing God's mission in the world move ahead with the mark of his character and nature.

Team life is not always like this. In fact, I would say that this kind of celebration as team is unique. It is a well-known fact – a key reason for attrition – that many people cease formal mission service because team life has collapsed. Others step away from living and serving in intentional missional communities or church families because of fractured relationships. There are myriad reasons for this, although often other causes are pointed to because the true reasons are too tender to speak about. Gospel living and service is hard, team life is hard, church life is often hard, and responding in a way that honours others and honours the Lord is hard. Sometimes we choose to protect ourselves at the cost of witness through interdependent community. The truth is that we all fail one another. The question is not *if* we will; it is *how* we will. The twin question should be, though: how will we choose to put on Christ's nature to identify ourselves as his? It is like a Scout uniform with a line of badges laid out for all to see, but in this case the badges are 'tenderhearted mercy, kindness, humility, gentleness, and patience', as they are listed in Colossians 3:12. 'These are the words, acts, attitudes that reveal Christ in us . . . signs, outward evidences of what is inward.'[5]

There have been times when I have felt diminished by colleagues and kept out of community – and I am sure I have made others feel the same. Sometimes the hurt people caused me was unintentional, or a splash of their own fears or thoughtlessness. At other times it was very intentional and very painful. 'Choose to believe the best of others,' we tell our people in sessions on team. Most of us do not wake up thinking we want to hurt someone, that we want to shape them for the worse. That is not our heart's desire. It is when the behaviour loops into a pattern that the real harm can come. This is something to watch out for, to guard against, not only in the lives of others but also in our own life. Instead, how can we *choose* life-giving behaviour, which really is God's love lived out to others? Without it, it is as though a house alarm has been triggered, its high-pitched screech grating on our ears, a modern version of the clanging cymbal from 1 Corinthians 13:1.

Formation questions

1 How have you been shaped by those you have served alongside?
2 Perhaps some of this shaping has been through hurtful, harmful experiences, ones you do not want to replicate. Note these down.
3 Do you need to forgive anyone for how they have harmed you as a colleague, or as a leader? Conversely, from whom do you need to seek forgiveness?
4 Hopefully, many have been through life-giving experiences which bring joy and consolidate commitment. What are those formational experiences for you?
5 When you think of putting on the uniform – character and nature – of Christ, which characteristics do you readily practise? Which characteristics need to be developed further?
6 How can we reproduce healthy, God-honouring, gospel communities that bear witness to others?

14

Formed from . . . those we serve

Recipients or teachers?

Like many others, as I prepared for engagement in joining God's work in the world in a nation other than my home country, a vision developed. I wanted to serve the animist poor in an urban centre. That reshaped into desiring to serve the poor among the teeming, mostly Hindu, millions of an urban megacity. I wanted to change the world, or change their world, at least. Little did I know the lasting impact this collection of women and children would have on my own life.

A colleague of mine, Peter, talks about how cross-cultural mission workers often view those they serve as objects of mission, their own or someone else's. We come with our education, our wealth, our passion to fix, bring change, with a touch of innocent superiority tucked away in our back pocket. Then we leave. Our work is done. We can dust off our hands and get on with our lives. Ajith Fernando adds another layer to this, writing:

> We have found that many people . . . are not prepared for the frustration of being servants of a struggling people. They come looking for the best package. They are not ready to die; they are not prepared for the frustration they will surely encounter. Their understanding of fulfillment is a worldly one that looks at it in terms of how they can best use their abilities and talents rather than how they can best be servants of God and the people.[1]

Subconsciously, perhaps, we at times become the centre of our own service, seeking fulfilment or belonging or justification or purpose through loving and helping others. We download ourselves in a way, pouring out our gifts, our knowledge, our resources for the sake of others, even, perhaps, if those we serve do not want to receive in quite that way. We create a separation between us and them – the server and the served – whoever the 'us' and 'them' may be. We hold back from incarnating ourselves in a self-emptying manner, truly sharing life and friendship in organic and earthy ways so that the line between server and served is blurred and the exchange becomes mutual rather than one-directional.

Add to this the high value that many missional people place on methodology, a system of performing a task to better achieve a result. This often 'depicts people merely as a means to an end'.[2] But Jesus broke any such rules, stepping beyond the traditional societal norms in meeting the Samaritan woman at the well, for example. He saw others as unique and worthy of encounters outside accepted rubrics and methods.

Seeing others as objects of mission is a distorted way of seeing the world, of seeing mission, as though looking through curved glass. I have fallen into that way of thinking, and it must have wounded God's heart, where each one of us is made in his image, precious in his sight. The same approach is witnessed in other variations: mission workers going out to minister but withdrawing into their expatriate teams to play or enjoy fellowship, their closest friends being those who echo their world view, their values. Or perhaps a mutual respect has developed between expatriate and national, whichever cultural mix that may entail, but the relationship shies away from real friendship, a true sense of family. Perhaps we have forgotten just how much we need each other, how those we have come to serve teach and give to us in return.

Shravya was one of my teachers, this strong, gracious, warm, Hindu-background leader in the slum. A trusted woman, she was one of our first points of contact in that community and soon became one of the literacy teachers. She was wise, patient and always welcoming. I still remember the day when the two of us went to visit another woman. With the railway tracks stretching behind us, Shravya quietly took my hand in hers as we walked together in friendship. 'I belong now,' I thought. 'I belong a little bit more now.' This woman, so faithful, so trustworthy, also knew pain. Her alcoholic husband would regularly beat her, the blue-grey bruises deepening her already dark skin. Holding her one day as she wept, I thought: 'When was the last time she was held gently or touched in kindness?' We were bound together across divides of language, culture, religion, education, economic status. Two women, loved and created by the God of all things, worthy and wanted by him.

Or Kashvi, Hindu by religion and name, who was pushed to the margins of her husband's family, especially once he had died. Crippled by polio as a child, she would limp through the slum, calling out greetings to others, her face split with a smile, joy bubbling over.

Or fiery, fierce Ridhi, who was incredibly clever, probably ending up as a lawyer had she had the opportunity of education when she was younger. She was quick – quick to learn, quick to defend, loyal to those who belonged to her. A woman to be seen, really seen, with dignity and purpose, in the midst of crowds and noise.

Or shy, quiet, brave Chara. Her husband used to keep her locked up 'for safety' while he worked. Once she became pregnant, on the doctor's demand that she get more sun, her husband allowed her to go up to the roof. Over time his grip loosened, and she came to the literacy programme, then the income-generation programme, leaving the slum in the company of others, earning her own money for the first time in her life. It was Chara who took the first loan through our shared micro-economic scheme. It was Chara who built a small brick home back in the village. It was Chara who embodied fortitude and courage, long-term thinking and committed financial planning. It was Chara, and her little daughter, Advika, who brought a calm peace to our group.

All of these women, and more, were my teachers. I had come to bring change, transformation. If that happened in embryonic or lasting ways, it was by God's grace, Christ's power, the Spirit's move and leadership. What I do know is that these women were a part of my own formation. They continue, even a decade later, to give me perspective (even the most rigid of Covid lockdowns pales in comparison to slum life) and to inform my choices, especially those around lifestyle. Their fortitude and resilience have been an example to me time and again. Their stories and pictures speak of the gift of their life, unseen by many, but full of dignity, worth and grace to those who are paying attention.

My mind moves to those currently in my sphere of influence. Yes, I lead or teach or invest in them. Yet, as I read this person's essay, I am formed because they see the world differently from me. As I observe or overhear or interact with people during a leadership development session, I am deepened because a different culture or gender or experience has sculpted their response. As I hear about someone's wrestle to remain mentally healthy, or about their marriage struggle, team dynamics or understanding of church, I continue to be shaped, as together we turn to the shaper of all, the Spirit of God. The formational influence of others, particularly those we serve, is a bounty discovered, a mutual exchange of gifts. We hear questions we would not ask ourselves. We view a discussion from varied angles. We are exposed to journeys vastly different from our own. If the influence is one-directional, something is missing. If we take nothing away from an encounter with another, something is lost.

If we were to gather together a group of people preparing for engagement in God's mission in the world and brainstorm the characteristics that would enrich their outward-focused gospel lives and communities, we would fill a whiteboard with a range of important qualities. They might include prayerfulness, being a person of God's word, flexibility, valuing team, being faith-filled and faithful, having a love and respect for cultures other than their own, being comfortable with the uncomfortable, and so on. You could add another good handful, I am sure. A characteristic often overlooked, though, but vital nonetheless, is teachability. Some mission organisations or gospel groups 'look for teachability as the most important character quality'[3] as they expand their community. Remaining teachable, no matter how old or young, how experienced or confident, sure or insecure, reflects the humble, gentle Spirit of Jesus. It is this posture that guards against objectifying anyone we serve, no matter how tired we are on that day or how long we have been in a role.

It is about more than just loving someone. We can love those we serve and still see them as objects of mission. They can still be the recipients of what we have to give. We can still be the ones controlling the relationship in one way or another, the ones holding the power. But as we lower ourselves to a shared picnic rug, or sit around a collective table, with no specific person acting as host, then something mysterious happens – we are invited into the mutuality of God's mission. Though the World Council of Churches is referring to God's empowerment of the Church in its 'Together towards Life' statement, this quote brings alive the image of a shared table:

> God's hospitality calls us to move beyond . . . [the] notion of culturally dominant groups as hosts and migrant and minority peoples as guests. Instead, in God's hospitality, God is host and we are all invited by the Spirit to participate with humility and mutuality in God's mission.[4]

Broaden that image out to see God extending his hospitality to all people – giver and recipient alike. Then, together, we come empty-handed to God's table, receiving from him as host. It is a powerful reminder to treasure humility, teachability and self-emptying as together we receive from the true giver of all, and through him, from one another. Such a posture is an unexpected yet exquisite expression of dependence on God and humility before others as we live out our love for him to those around us.

Formation questions

1 How have those you have served also been your teachers?
2 What of Christ do you recognise in the people you have served? How do you need them?
3 Have you fallen into the trap of viewing people as 'objects of mission'?
4 Consider the picture of coming to a table where God is host. What is happening in your heart, your mind, your imagination?
5 Do you see yourself as teachable? If so, how? Or why not?
6 How can you continue to grow in humility, in teachability, in the area of emptying yourself?

Part 3

LIFELONG FORMATION: STRENGTHENING OUR INNER BEING

Formation water wheel

We are formed *by* the Spirit, formed *through* the powerful and intimate pathway of prayer, formed *for* the earthy and sacred purpose of Jesus-centred, outward-focused gospel witness, and formed *from* multiple materials that leave their mark on us. Formation is a recurring process, like a water wheel going through its cycles: catching water, emptying water, being filled, spilling out. It is a continuous, lifelong process. It is a covenant journey with the Spirit as we move ahead with intentional fidelity and surrender. 'Come, Lord Jesus,' we cry, 'keep forming me, keep forming us! Form us for a lifestyle characteristic of you and your heart that longs to draw others into life-giving relationship with yourself.'

Throughout his writings, the apostle Paul's warm love and deep commitment to the various communities and churches he had invested in is easily evident. He sends greetings; he encourages his audience and glows with pride; he rebukes and challenges those in his spiritual family. His genuine desire and motivation are that these scattered groups of believers will follow Jesus more closely, reflecting the family likeness of Christ their brother and God their Father. Paul longed for every one of these church members to grow up in Christ, maturing and strengthening into spiritual adults. In some ways his prayer for the church at Ephesus (Ephesians 3:14–19) summarises his heartfelt cry for all those entrusted to him. The New International Version uses several words that would be helpful for us to consider together:

> For this reason I kneel before the Father, from whom every family in heaven and on earth derives its name. I pray that out of his glorious riches he may strengthen you with power

through his Spirit in your inner being, so that Christ may dwell in your hearts through faith. And I pray that you, being rooted and established in love, may have power, together with all the Lord's holy people, to grasp how wide and long and high and deep is the love of Christ, and to know this love that surpasses knowledge – that you may be filled to the measure of all the fullness of God.

There is so much contained in these few verses, more than we can examine here. However, one thing Paul sees the need for is a continual strengthening of the inner being of those who follow Jesus – in this case, the members of the Ephesian church. He prays for power in their inner being, their inner self, their interior places of formation. It is an evolving work gifted out of the Father's immeasurable and holy treasures and implemented by the Spirit. This strengthening work is done so that 'all things Jesus' may take hold in us with roots that will go deep into the soil of love, watered by faith, bearing the fruit of power, beautified by the flowers of the fullness of God. It is Paul's wholehearted prayer for those he loves and leads, that they may enter more deeply into the revealed mysteries of God. He wants them to grasp the true dimensions of Christ's love, like stepping out of a two-dimensional painting and into the fuller three dimensions, suddenly having a vast world revealed to them. He longs for this depth to fill them to the brim with all that God has for them. Filling up and spilling out.

It is not easy to be a person who seeks to belong wholly and solely to Jesus, shaped by the Spirit to point others to the Father. It takes faithfulness and fortitude, resolve and resilience, strong and supple inner beings, intention and integrity. These are aspects, among others, that we need to purposefully mature in, like the spiritual 'lego' of 2 Peter 1:5–8, in which the various characteristics of the Spirit connect to and enhance the next characteristic. Being gospel-orientated means having a Jesus-centred worldview and biblical values, making God-honouring choices in how we use our lives and how we respond to interactions and events throughout the day, seeing all spheres of life and engagement as opportunities for bearing witness to the name and person of Jesus. It is a privileged challenge, an open-ended invitation into God-at-work-in-the-world.

As a mind, expanded by a new idea, never returns to its old shape (to paraphrase Oliver Wendell Holmes), so too with us, as we develop as God's outward-focused people. Our character stretches; our nature morphs; our capacity is enlarged; our ability to respond to stress and struggle and sorrow and suffering grows. All of this provides a constellation of opportunities to live out Christ. These changes can bring calcification, or, if kneaded by the Spirit, they are made elastic.

Some time ago I drove to a coastal pier near the house where I was spending a few months. It was a bright, sunshiny winter's day. The water was clear and light jade in colour, although still full of swollen waves rolling into the sandy shoreline. Standing at the end of the jetty, I watched the water curl in, crashing into the bottom of the walkway, a foot or two below where I stood. Turning, I looked along the narrow corridor of pylons, the water splashing against those sturdy legs. Life was growing around the pillars: seaweed twisting with the sea's forceful motion, barnacles suctioned on, coral clinging tightly. This place is home to three species of seahorses, multiple fish, and other marine life. It is a sheltered habitat for a range of sea life, a protected harbour throughout the seasons and varied weather.

That is the paradox of seeing the Spirit develop our inner being – the need to be sturdy, steadfast, sure, and yet to be flexible, agile, with the ability to bounce back and remain hopeful, trusting. Perhaps it is more like earthquake-proof buildings that can survive shock and subterranean movement from unexpected places and at unexpected times.

Over the years, as I have called four nations home, lived, worked, laughed, cried, listened to, learned from, taught, mentored, invested in, been astounded by, been hurt, caused hurt, forgiven and been forgiven, grown and grown up, led and seen people shaped by the Spirit's working, there have been a handful of consistent areas, regular patterns, where I and others have needed deeper formation. They are trails to follow as we continue to 'strengthen our inner being'. Some are more obscure than others, but all are worth prayerfully considering as we choose to look more like Jesus each day. These are areas we are formed *to* engage in, setting us apart as outward-focused Jesus-people.

15

Formed to . . . trust

Choosing to trust God

'Is he trustworthy?' Sometimes that question is asked of God; other times it is about a person – he or she. Trusting someone, even God, is easy to do in our heads, but can be difficult to do in our hearts, in the fabric of our lives. The core of it, though, comes back to our relationship with the Lord and how much we trust him, trust that he is good. Not just good, but good to us. Those words from the Lord to exiled Israel – 'For I know the plans I have for you . . . plans to prosper you and not to harm you, plans to give you hope and a future' (Jeremiah 29:11 NIV) – are often thrown around with bumper-sticker ease. However, as we apply them to our own lives, we may find that it is a lot easier to believe that God will not harm us than it is to believe that he has good things for us. He is good, absolutely. But is he good to us, to me?

God's goodness, though, is wrapped up in relationship. The following verses point out how Israel's answer came through close relationship with God (Jeremiah 29:12–14a NIV):

- 'Then you will call on me and come and pray to me . . .' Call. Come. Pray. *Movement towards God.*
- '. . . and I will listen to you.' *God's movement towards us.*
- 'You will seek me and find me when you seek me with all your heart.' Seek. Wholeheartedly. Find. *Movement towards God.*
- 'I will be found by you,' the Lord answers. *God's movement towards his people.*

This dynamic drawing together of God and his people, reflecting covenant relationship, is a way of knowing and being known. That is the basis of the goodness out of which his practical provisions emerge or reform. God is trustworthy. His reliability is a part of his character, his nature. He is worthy of our trust. The difficulty comes when our spiritual cataracts and foggy minds limit what form that trust should take. At times we feel that he has torn our trust because of what should or should not have been allowed to happen in our lives.

So often when we talk about the promises of God, we talk about the positive elements, which are many. His goodness abounds. Yet one of his promises is that life will not be easy. We should expect hard times, trouble, crisis, especially if we identify as followers of Jesus. That, too, in the illogical logic of heaven, is also good, because it pulls us tightly into the embrace of Christ's suffering. We may know this theologically, but unless we can integrate this knowledge, we find ourselves spinning from lost hope and crumbling trust in response to hardship.

Just after the beginning of time, the world was marred, and we have been dealing with the consequences ever since. As gospel-centred people, as we go to bring hope and life and liberty into this hurting world, we are stirring up a hornet's nest of enemy assault. Expect hardship, trouble, crisis, say the writers of Romans and James, among other biblical authors. The question is: what will that suffering look like and how will we stay supernaturally open in the midst of it?

Most of us have learned the lesson that life is not easy. We have been bumped and bruised, stabbed or beaten up, crushed or reduced in one way or another. We have experienced loss, grief or suffering. If hardship has not come, it will, in whatever shape or form that may take. Just give it time. Some of us may not feel that we can question God, shake our fist in disappointment, anger, hurt or confusion. I say this carefully, respectfully, on holy ground:

really, God is big enough for that. Your anger or confusion does not take him by surprise. It is not as though he cannot handle the wildness of your emotion. It does not push him off balance or cause him to step back offended, holding his hands up to ward off the fire of your words. After all, David is brutally candid with God in the Psalms, questioning him in Psalm 13, and expressing his frustration, even anger, in Psalm 109, to mention just two. God, our Father and Saviour, is graciously present. He is the come-alongside-Immanuel-God. He sits with us, during the tantrums, the ache, the utter bewilderment, the murky mist, the questions. Anger is part of grief, and grief expresses loss. Processing our pain allows us to journey through the dark tunnel and eventually come out the other end.

Lament is an important part of this – where, fiercely honest and raw before God, we expose the corners of ourselves to him. This is especially hard, but important, when life has turned grey. We lay it all bare – anger and ache, bitterness and betrayal, confusion and complaint, pain and persecution, hurt and harm, weariness and wounds. We say with passion, 'This is life right now and I hate it,' or some alternative thereof. We cry our variation of Psalm 13, filled with questions, surrendering in emptiness. We echo Jeremiah 29:12. We call, come, pray. We invite God to show up. We cling to him despite our shattered hearts.

In the end it is a matter of trusting that God is really, truly, present in the sadness of broken reality; that he is good, and good to us, to each one of his kids. Kidnapping or miscarriage, rape, or never finding a marriage partner, organisational racism or war, missional poverty or cancer. He is God. And he is good – to us, even when that is the last thing it feels like.

I have been journeying with a dear friend over the last few years. This belief that God is good and that we have the choice to trust has been tested by her time and again. She was mired in a situation that had dragged on for months, wearing down her resolve and endurance, affecting her mental health and ability to bounce back. During that time, she had good days and bad days, but we were in it together. Sometimes we need to choose trust as an act of will. 'Today I choose to trust. Tomorrow I will choose to trust. The next day I will choose to trust' – until it sinks into habit. For her, choosing to trust meant engaging with God, who turned and turns his face towards her, and choosing to turn towards him in return. It looked like responding to his invitation to go deeper into his heart, no matter how exhausted she was on any given day. It manifested in clasping his hand tightly as he led her one step at a time through the confusion and the unknown. It was throwing herself on him in desperation, and calling on others to faithfully fight for and repeatedly pray with her. It was expressed in being vulnerable to and dependent on others, trusting that God was working through them as well. She has been formed through that time. Her inner being was strengthened, like the slow building of her core muscles. Her prayer life changed shape. Rather than always caring for others, she has learned to allow others to care for her. Trust for her is not only God-orientated but also lived out communally. And when the temptation revisits to think that she is alone, she chooses to believe Jesus' words of truth: 'I am always with you' (see Matthew 28:20), and to believe that he has surrounded her with people who love and are committed to her. She has experienced a myriad of expressions of God's faithfulness in her life and does not want to forget. Her hope comes from his consistent faithfulness, his unchanging character, and she desires to reflect this back to him. During the height of that particular situation, she decided each day to remember his goodness and retain hope, and she continues to do so now. It is not an easy choice. It tests her resolve. In *Resilience in Life and Faith*, the authors write:

God seems to allow situations to arise that expose our own inability to cope and cause us to grow in our dependency upon him. We are never stronger than when we are most conscious of our own inadequacy yet leaning on the dependability of God in any and every circumstance.[1]

Today my friend chooses to trust. Tomorrow she will choose to trust. The next day she will choose to trust, until it sinks into habit.

In the past I have had to remind myself to choose trust, particularly when Immanuel – 'God with us' – seemed absent. He was not, of course, but he *felt* absent, as if he had turned his face away from me, forgotten me in his silence. My knowledge of who he is and my experience of him were disjointed, disappointing, at times torn apart through excruciating pain. But

dark times can be pregnant with God's purpose; they can be times in which we are stripped of our overdependence on the emotional life, on the things of this world, and on ourselves. 'The dark night' [as some refer to it] is one of the ways the Spirit slows our pace, even bringing us to a halt, so that he can work an inner transformation of the heart and soul. Those who are hungry for God can expect to be drawn or driven into times of dryness or confusion, where faith and dependence on God are tested and deepened. You will learn for yourself what all the schools in the world could not teach you – the healing action of faith without supporting pleasure.[2]

It was like that during my final year in Southeast Asia. I had gone out of the country for a break, during which time the Lord made it very clear that it was time for me to hand over my responsibilities in our team ministry. As I began working on the various phases of handover, I was asking the Lord what was next. He remained silent, for months and months and months. I was reading Isaiah that year. For chapter after chapter, God remained silent. The book was filled with rich truths, for sure, but nothing seemed to resonate or reverberate. My thinking and emotions were divided. I had to come back to what I knew to be truth – the knowledge part of theology – and wait for my hurting, confused heart to catch up, and for God's silence to break.

Andrew Peterson's song 'The Silence of God' (Essential Records, 2003) speaks into this experience profoundly, with expressive characteristics and qualities. It is a silence that may be absent of sound, but is swollen with God's presence. It is a silence that is desolate and solitary, and yet strangely hallowed. The drumbeat of grief may set in, but the unravelling finally halts. Hope lingers in the sacred, lonely richness of God's echoing silence.

God can use words, of course, as Ken Gire reminds us, but often 'it seems He speaks without them. Not because He can't speak or because we can't hear, but because words are often the least effective way of communicating.'[3]

At some point the silence lifts and the waiting is over.

Waiting is an important element of our formation process, especially regarding hardship and suffering. The God of infinite patience values waiting, teaching us lessons that slowly work their way down into the marrow of our bones. He waits with us, patiently sitting beside us until we realise that he has been there all along, holding, loving, preparing, redeeming our pain. We wait and wait, bearing his silence – because there 'are some things God can accomplish with His tenderness over time that He cannot accomplish with His power in a moment'.[4] Time and waiting are yoked together for the Spirit's shaping purposes.

Hopefully, though, we are not just bearing and enduring. Hopefully, we are also 'developing patient attentiveness to the ways that holiness develops over a lifetime, which necessarily includes stretches of boredom and pain and suffering, which Dorothy Day named "the long loneliness"'.[5]

It took forty long chapters of Isaiah before the Lord broke his silence all those years ago. I was up in a northern state of the country I was living in, attending the wedding of a dear friend's brother. The day before the wedding I was sitting outside on a bench, reading Isaiah 40. Coming to verse 11, I read:

He will feed his flock like a shepherd.
   He will carry the lambs in his arms,
holding them close to his heart.
   He will gently lead the mother sheep with their young.

Looking up, I saw Nirmala with her baby boy tied to her chest with a large swathe of cloth, the wide band nestling her son tightly against her. The words 'He will carry . . . them close to his heart' suddenly turned from black and white to vivid colour, bringing tears of relief to my eyes.

Sharing this with a friend years later, he paused, commenting: 'It is interesting, isn't it, that the Lord would trust you with his silence?' *Trust me with his silence.* It is certainly not something I would choose to be trusted with, but rather than fighting or rejecting it, I want to learn to receive it and steward his silence well.

Yesterday I was walking along the beach, the waves turning to foam as they licked the shore. It had been raining all day, a steady deluge. Finally, the rain had stopped, allowing me to make an escape and stretch my legs. The sky remained grey, heavy with the promise of more rain. The sea was murky, dulled by the muted heavens above, and yet a tinge of green and blue shone from the waters, subdued, for sure, but still present.

As we wait out the silence of God, choosing to trust, we can do so in hope, spotting the tinges of promise as they shine through. The benediction towards the end Paul's letter to the Romans points to this: 'I pray that God, the source of hope, will fill you completely with joy and peace because you trust in him. Then you will overflow with confident hope through the power of the Holy Spirit' (Romans 15:13). This is the hope that bears fruit through the supernatural working of the Spirit, embedded in the earthiness and messiness of our lives.

The word 'hope' here – *elpis* in Greek – is key. It does not mean hope in the way that we so often use it: hoping that we will do well in our exams or that Covid will finally disappear, that our marriage will turn around, or that life will right itself after a deep wrong has been done or felt. We use the word 'hope' more like a wish or a desire, a strong wanting.

This Greek term, *elpis*, implies much more. It ties together expectation and surety, a pledge of assurance proven by Jesus' death. This hope is found in the person of Christ (1 Timothy 1:1).[6] It is something we can rest in with confidence, despite lacking clarity (Hebrews 11:1).[7] This hope is being sure of the promises that we know to be true, expressed in a myriad of Scripture passages[8] and a myriad of ways. We can be certain of them, even though they so often remain hidden or look like a distant outline on a far-off mountain ridge. This hope anchors us, helping us to remain firm and secure as the currents and storms of this life bring imbalance. It is not something that will shift with our whim, or change with our desires. It will not fall apart with a pandemic or financial crisis or our own unique ache. It is that way because our God is that way. We can hold on to this hope because 'God can be trusted to keep his promise' (Hebrews 10:23). This hope is earthy, relevant, resolute, and it helps strengthen our inner being as we, his representatives, are formed into the likeness of Christ for the sake of this world he loves.

Although she is not writing within the context of a theology of risk and suffering, Brené Brown adds insight into this area of cultivating hope. She writes:

I found in my research that men and women who self-report as hopeful put considerable value on persistence and hard work. The new cultural belief that everything should be fun, fast, and easy is inconsistent with hopeful thinking. It also sets us up for hopelessness. When we experience something that is difficult and requires significant time and effort, we are quick to think, This is supposed to be easy; it's not worth the effort, or, This should be easier: it's only hard and slow because I'm not good at it. Hope . . . sounds more like, This is tough, but I can do it.[9]

As believers, we know that the source of our hope is Christ himself. This reminder that an other-orientated gospel life will be difficult helps to set the framework as we join God's mission in the world. We know it will require significant time and effort, even significant sacrifice and pain. With a humble posture of expectancy and responsiveness, we depend on the source, the God of hope, who fills us up so that we can spill out to others.

Formation questions

1 How have you grappled with your theology of suffering, integrating your knowledge of God, and the promise that life in him will not be easy, with the earthiness of your reality?
2 Examine the assumptions resulting from your theology of suffering. Are those assumptions biblical? If not, what is the source?
3 In what ways does your gospel community promote a sound theology of suffering?
4 How are you choosing or not choosing to trust the Lord?
5 What is your experience of the silence of God? What did you learn through that time?
6 What place do the following have in your life: hardship, blessing, waiting, hope?

16

Formed to . . . be open

Choosing to trust others

Years ago, a friend and I were out in the ocean in a blow-up dinghy. It was a glorious day, sunny and warm. We dragged the boat into the shallows, hopped in and began floating away. We talked and laughed and played. Then we realised where we were. We were far out, unknowingly pulled into the depths. We grabbed the paddles and got to work, but still, we made little progress. The current was too strong, and we were too inexperienced and weak. Finally, others noticed and sent out a boat to haul us back in, much to our relief. We had a lot to learn about reading and riding on the ocean's currents.

An aspect of growing up and letting go, of continuing formation, is the ability to progressively navigate the unknown waters and their various undercurrents, not so much of the open sea, as above, but of life expressed through relationship. We refine our awareness of and capacity to hold disparate, contrasting realities together before we are swept away into dangerous deep waters.

Some time back I had an 'a-ha' moment. It was caused by a combination of reading a novel by an extremely creative and eloquent author and watching a cross-cultural situation unfold in a meeting. The author likened thinking about two disparate ideas to singing harmony with yourself – seemingly impossible, irreconcilable. The meeting demanded we hold the opposing past and present realities together so as to move into the future. To deny one reality or the other would be neither respectful nor helpful. There was a sense of discord, murky confusion, as well as humility as we sought to steward this delicate situation.

So often we want to understand something (or someone) fully before we can move on. Those of us who come from nations where logical, scientific educational systems are the norm want to know *why*; we want the reason. That is not always possible, especially as we become more comfortable with the mysteries of God.

One of the cultural dimensions that Geert Hofstede[1] established is *uncertainty avoidance*: learning to cope well with the unpredictable, uncertain, uncontrollable. It is an area of development encountered when maturing our cultural intelligence, but it is also an area of lifelong formation broader than cultural intelligence. As we become more flexible and adaptable, we learn to let go of control and become at peace with that which we cannot predict. As we become more and more agile in our ability to pivot when unforeseen circumstances arise, we become more resilient. In his book *The Servant-Leader Within*, Robert Greenleaf wrote: 'I began to learn to be comfortable with moving into the unknown with confidence.'[2] As we engage with new opportunities and contexts, and enter cultural or relational complexities, we can hold disparate ideas together. We learn to navigate murky waters, despite the pull of the undercurrent, with growing confidence. In the background, the root of our growing resilience, is the quiet certainty that we can trust in the One who holds us throughout all this ambiguity.

During the initial years of Covid, it felt as though the yo-yo of multiple lockdowns was teaching us how to respond to the uncontrollable. It caused us to pivot, hopefully with grace and growing ease. It strengthened the core muscles of our inner being rather than allowing them to turn flabby. I wonder: did it work? Did we surround this experience in prayer so that we reacted and will continue to react in Spirit-like ways? Or did we just want to lie down for a while and leave the adapting to others, waiting for it to pass?

Closely tied to the idea of disparity and uncertainty is that of expectations or expectancy, responsibility or response. When rereading William Young's *The Shack*, I stumbled on an interesting discussion between Mack, the main character, and Sarayu, the name Young gives to the Holy Spirit as a character within the book. Regardless of your reaction to *The Shack*, the following idea is helpful as we consider the continuous formation process.

Sarayu is explaining how expectancy and the ability to respond are full of life, full of possibility, engaging and vibrant, made to be lived out in relationship with God himself and to spill out into relationship with others in profound and unique ways. 'If I simply gave you a *responsibility*, I would not have to be with you at all. It would now be a task to perform, an obligation to be met, something to fail.'[3] Sarayu continues:

> Mack, if you and I are friends, there is an expectancy that exists within our relationship. When we see each other or are apart, there is expectancy of being together, of laughing and talking. That expectancy has no concrete definition; it is alive and dynamic and everything that emerges from our being together is a unique gift shared by no one else. But what happens if I change that 'expectancy' to an 'expectation' – spoken or unspoken? Suddenly, law has entered into our relationship. You are now expected to perform in a way that meets my expectations. Our living friendship rapidly deteriorates into a dead thing with rules and requirements. It is no longer about you and me, but about what friends are supposed to do . . . the responsibility of a . . . friend.[4]

So often, our expectations of ourselves, our teammates, our church or missional community, our culture or work environment, become a weight where performance and requirements steal our sense of expectancy. The seriousness of responsibility becomes more important than how we respond to God and our neighbour. Nurturing a sense of expectancy and examining our responses can go a long way to maturing us into the likeness of Christ for the sake of others. It allows us to both regularly receive from and give grace to others.

It is often when we learn to let go and become more comfortable with the uncertain, when we trade expectations for expectancy, that we find ourselves expressing greater authenticity and vulnerability.

My dad has been working with his hands for years now. They have become calloused in places, with even some of his fingerprints wearing thin. Consequently, the sensitivity in his fingers has lessened. Each one of us can have our cultural or relational callouses, our theological or personal build-up where we have sought to protect ourselves. Heifetz and Linsky give this illustration in their book *Leadership on the Line*, encouraging us to retain 'innocence and wonder, doubt and curiosity, compassion and love in the hardest of times'.[5] We are vulnerable when we choose not to protect ourselves but instead are willing to consider why we are responding in a certain way. We are vulnerable when we accept and deal with difficult emotions or, in their words, 'to feel everything . . . to hold it all . . . and yet stay open'.[6]

But what does vulnerability look like? How can we assess our level of vulnerability?

It takes self-awareness and emotional intelligence, the ability to admit, recognise, filter and respond to your inner responses in a way that, as followers of Jesus, honours God and honours others. A thought or feeling may float or leap to the surface, and rather than just ignoring it or putting up a defensive emotional wall to others, we examine it before God the Spirit. It takes courage to peel back the mask and reveal our own weaknesses or failures or sin. It takes trust, of God and others, to offer our incomplete, broken selves without knowing if we will be accepted in that particular shape or at that particular time. However, the 'secret lies not in avoiding life's inevitable frustrations and upsets but in learning to recover from them'.[7]

Some time ago I was leading a week-long leadership development process. Although not ideal, we had to shift our face-to-face residential missional formation experience to an online platform as we were still in lockdown. To enrich this time, we introduced a segment called Learning through Story, where, each morning, one of our leaders would share a portion of their story that linked to the theme of the day. Every day, I came away aware of having stood on holy ground. These men and women made themselves vulnerable, displaying their imperfections for the sake of others. They were aware. They were courageous. They were trusting.

It is a holy thing to stay open when you have been betrayed or experienced trauma, when high stress or distress almost seem the norm, when others have failed you or you have failed them. It is a holy response to forgive when it is not humanly deserved, to trust again when belief has been fractured, to love when you are not wanted. It is counterintuitive, not normal. It is a work of the Spirit in a people who care more about honouring God than protecting themselves.

One of the most difficult aspects of being committed to God's community is choosing to trust others, remaining open and curious and willing to love in a way that echoes Jesus. Interestingly and anecdotally, when I first headed overseas to live as an adult, it seemed as though there was the assumption of trust. Team members or missional communities would trust one another until trust was torn. Now, though, it seems as though a shift has occurred, that there is often a hesitation to trust until community members earn that trust. This may be reflective of a greater number of divided families, or people having experienced the bullying or the cruelty we often observe on social media. Maybe. However, choosing to trust and hope in God also means choosing to trust others. Not those intent on evil but rather those in our gospel communities or teams, with their own idiosyncrasies and traits, lacking perfection and messing up, as you and I do. This choosing – to believe, to stay open, to trust – reflects the hope of Christ, even when it takes all our courage.

Many years ago, I was a part of a small missional community. It soon became evident that it was not the ideal team that I had longed for. Those who received me brought vast baggage into their leadership role, and for whatever confusing reason I was not wanted. My longing for community was met with doors firmly closed towards deeper relationship. I was implicitly and explicitly encouraged to choose independence over dependency, self-sufficiency over what could be interpreted as neediness. I had been warned that it would be like this, but in my earnestness the truth did not sink in until I met it head-on, outside my normal support structures. It was a lonely introduction to a new country. Innocent mistakes were made on multiple sides, including by me. The Lord kindly built my support base through other like-minded people. I was forced to turn to him more quickly because at times there was simply no one else. Mentors encouraged me to remain faithful even during those days when it felt like wading through mud. Through those early months, I learned to enjoy the fellowship of the Holy Spirit in new and real ways, and I began to value and rely on friendships with local people in this unfamiliar city. One thing the Lord reminded me of at the time, though, was that in the same way that he was still at work in me, he was at work in the lives of others on my team. Their behaviour, their choices, came from a place of reaction rather than responsiveness, from a history of brokenness that understandably shut them down rather than opened them up. Yet it is a profound witness when our lives are reformed, like *kintsugi*, the work of Japanese artisans who refashion fragmented pottery using gold, the cracks showing clearly and yet strikingly beautiful. As communities of God's people, we are invited to choose trust over wariness, openness over protection. Wisely, yes, but still reflecting the generosity of God.

Formation questions

1 How comfortable are you when matters are unclear, whether they be work, relationship matters or the future?

2 When was the last time you reacted badly in the face of the unpredictable, uncertain or uncontrollable? If you had your time again, how would you respond?

3 Do you find yourself leaning towards expectations and responsibilities, or do you live with a posture of expectancy and responsiveness?

4 In what ways are you accepting of human brokenness as a common experience and able to love others and yourself when this frailty is visible, rather than being overly condemning?

5 In what ways does your gospel community encourage a culture of openness, vulnerability and support as its members deal with their brokenness? Are you able to face and share uncomfortable feelings? If not, why not?

6 How are you choosing to trust others, even when others have let you down?

17

Formed to . . . forgive

Receiving and extending radical forgiveness

Forgiveness is arguably the most difficult aspect of living out the life of Christ. It is not usually the small stuff that is hard to forgive. It is easy to shrug something off, to overlook it and let it go if it is not hugely important and has not brought much pain or suffering. But it is supremely difficult when it is something that matters. Perhaps the hurt is raw and deep, or the injustice is real and has diminished you. Maybe the pain or conflict has gone on for too long, like a tooth slowly rotting at its root. Then forgiveness is a supernatural challenge, won only through the Spirit.

What we often forget is that forgiveness is the crux of the good news of Jesus Christ. Salvation history circles around the cross of Jesus Christ, from where forgiveness flows. Our broken and frayed relationship with the God of all things was knitted back together at the cross through Jesus' shed blood. Our purpose on earth is dependent on the cross; our always-future with God is given because of the cross. The cross is key. Forgiveness is fundamental. Without it, we have no hope to live by, as God's people.

The confounding truth is that it is the nature of God to extend forgiveness, to graciously erase the debts piled high, although, of course, only through Christ's costly payment. As we, his followers, his kids, are converted more and more into Christ's form, we are to live out his family likeness. This includes extending forgiveness with the same grace and generosity of spirit that we see in Jesus' acts of relational reconciliation. N. T. Wright, referring to early followers of Jesus, powerfully expounds on this:

In particular, having received God's forgiveness themselves, they were to practice it amongst themselves. Not to do so would mean they hadn't grasped what was going on. As soon as someone in one of these Jesus-cells refused to forgive a fellow-member, he or she was saying, in effect, 'I don't really believe the Kingdom has arrived. I don't think the Forgiveness of Sins has actually occurred.' Failure to forgive one another wasn't a matter of failing to live up to a new bit of moral teaching. It was cutting off the branch you were sitting on. The only reason for being Kingdom-people, for being Jesus' people, was that the forgiveness of sins was happening; so if you didn't live forgiveness, you were denying the very basis of your own new existence.[1]

That is an intense statement, a confronting one. We believe it in our heads, but oh, it is hard to live out in the muck and mire of our lives. But if we long to reflect the person, the story and the glory of the Christ we follow, our lives must be marked with the sign of forgiveness, both received and given.

We forgive to honour our Father, but we also do it as a wholehearted and authentic demonstration of following Jesus. It is an invitation into the lively work of the Spirit. Forgiveness is an act of worship and witness. In fact, as Henry French states, it

is central to the mission of God and the mission of God's people. In the cancellation of debt that cannot possibly be paid back, God provides the indebted with a new start, a new start characterized by the transformation of the radically forgiven into those who also radically forgive.[2]

Can you sense the Spirit of God at work in those words? We are transformed from being radically *forgiven* to being the radically *forgiving*. This marks us, characterises us, distinguishing us from others, stamping us as Jesus-people. We are called out for more.

It is not normal to forgive like that. It is human to harbour pain, to turn away from relationship when someone has hurt or shamed or not believed the best of us. It is human to blame others or make excuses or refuse to take responsibility. It is easy to interpret misunderstanding as truth or to allow our reactions and emotions to reign. That is natural for sinful and marred humans. However, we have the Trinity, who has moved into each one of our addresses and begun the work of renovation with the Spirit as site manager. A costly example has been set, an invitation sent out, a helper given. Forgiveness is offered *to* us; forgiveness is to be offered *by* us.

Why? Why would God expect this of us? Aside from the forgiveness petition tucked into the Lord's Prayer, there are two other Scripture passages in particular that remind us of the power of this radical forgiveness.

Step with me into the scene of Jesus on the cross. There are several prayers that Jesus uttered while he was on the cross, two of which Luke records. The first of these is found in Luke 23:34. Although some early manuscripts do not include this verse, it is accepted within church history and familiar to many of us: Jesus said, 'Father, forgive them, for they don't know what they are doing.' This phrase echoes a portion of the Lord's Prayer and sets the scene for Stephen's later prayer. Here we witness what Eugene Peterson names the 'recklessness and lavishness of Jesus' forgiveness'.[3] It is true! The forgiveness that Christ extends is illogical, lavish, upside down, seemingly foolish. He laid down all his money – his life – betting on humankind. It was risky, a display of holy recklessness, and yet the persons of the Trinitarian godhead knew exactly what they were doing. Jesus' years on earth, his public and private words, his miracles and acts of compassion, led to the supreme act of the cross. Here his speech and action crashed into each other in this prayer for forgiveness, the very foundation of Christian belief.

French continues dealing out profound and provocative words, noting that forgiveness 'undermines the structures of the kingdom of evil and establishes a new community . . . the coming kingdom of God'.[4] As outward-focused people who long to point others to Jesus, part of our engagement with the world is to see the enemy's work curtailed, his power and impact diminished, to be a part of the subversive undermining of his kingdom. This is the frontline of God's mission in the world, in whatever nation, among whichever people. We take the fight to the enemy by choosing radical forgiveness, costly though it may be.

The other powerful passage on forgiveness is set in the context of the early church in Acts, with Stephen as the main character. In Acts 6:1–6 he was recognised as one of those men whose life was flavoured by grace and faith, wisdom and the Spirit's empowerment. We soon read about the opposition he faced, and the story of his death. Emboldened by the Spirit, he made a zealous speech before the Jewish council, the Sanhedrin, which led to him becoming the first martyr of the early church. Spirit-filled, he peered into heaven, catching an unparalleled glimpse of God's glory and Jesus' place (Acts 6:8 – 7:56).

We read on: 'As they stoned him, Stephen prayed, "Lord Jesus, receive my spirit." He fell to his knees, shouting, "Lord, don't charge them with this sin!"' (Acts 7:59–60). As Paul stood watching and Stephen lay dying, Stephen echoed two of Jesus' prayers from the cross, including that of forgiving his enemies. It is a startling reaction, showing not so much a great presence of mind as an intrinsic alignment of spirit. Stephen was so abandoned to Jesus' way of doing things, even in his death, perhaps especially in his death, that this cry naturally slipped out in his last moments. Jesus' death on the cross was the background music to Stephen's own death scene, modelling the Christian life and death as a new way of forgiveness without payback, setting the tone for God's people to be a radically forgiving people.

C. S. Lewis wrote: 'To be a Christian means to forgive the inexcusable, because God has forgiven the inexcusable in you.'

The tricky part is doing it, because the truth is that it is easy to ignore growing bitterness. At first it is only a tiny seed, but before we know it a fully grown bush or tree has taken root. It is easy to ignore the unforgiveness that has moved into one of the rooms of our life, arriving as a visitor but morphing into a well-established member of the family. How do we know unforgiveness has taken up residence? Indicators can vary from continuing to think about the situation or person, allowing your thought-life to steal your joy. It can take a more active role where you seek to justify yourself to others or tarnish another person's reputation, ensuring that you look better after the telling of the story. It may arise when a sense of expectancy has curdled into stiff expectation, or when responsiveness has hardened into rigid responsibility. Just as PeaceWise[5] encourages, genuine forgiveness only happens when our heart-issues are resolved before God and others. Then the more 'surface' matters can be sustainably reconciled. When we trust God, working with him to discover his goodness in this or that particular situation; when we remain open, even when we have been hurt by others, forgiveness wins.

Some time ago two separate events occurred concurrently, each causing a depth of grief I had not experienced for years. Combined, it was as if a pervading ache had moved in, made itself comfortable and decided to stay for a while. One of these events blindsided me, bringing a confusion of emotion: surprise, betrayal, vulnerability, fear. For the first week I felt unbalanced, off-kilter, as if that proverbial rug had been yanked hard and sent my feet flying. Objectively, I could see what was happening and why it was happening, but still, those fat, silent tears kept brimming over. Humanly, it would have been so easy to become bitter, for my heart to harden and to break relationship, but I so longed to honour the Lord in my response. It was a battle, a long wrestle, and it took time. It took time to grieve, to readjust, to hear from the Lord and see his perspective. It took time to trust with my heart and not just my head. It took time so that I could celebrate that even this 'thing', once sad, was now glad. It was my own paltry Gethsemane moment, where I was reminded at the most visceral of levels that temptation and difficulty are conquered through 'persistent, intense, submissive prayer'.[6] There was a cost to the forgiveness. I had to remain silent about certain things so as not to tarnish anyone's name. I could not explain myself or even seek help from certain corners. It was humanly lonely, but the community of the Trinity opened their embrace and sojourned with me. Then something happened: an apology of sorts from the person who had caused this hurt. Not in words but in action. I read it that way, anyway. It was as if that person was saying, 'I see how difficult and painful this has been. Here is an offering.' It was unexpected and so helpful. And with that, any remnant of ache fled, any residue of unforgiveness evaporated.

The other situation is different. I still find hurt and related sadness floating to the surface at unexpected times over this matter. These feelings remind me to surrender it to the Lord again, to forgive and release again, to beg the Spirit to keep shining his light and doing his persistent work of formation within me . . . again. I am also reminded that I can only be responsible for my own responses, not that of the other person. I can keep seeking to reflect the character of Christ even when they forget to or choose not to. Wrapped up in forgiveness within this situation is releasing expectations while retaining hope. I forgive the inexcusable or hurtful because that too has been forgiven in me.

We receive forgiveness, swept away by God's tsunami of grace. We receive it. We believe it. How can we not extend it to others? This cornerstone of our faith has etched on to us the mark of Jesus' witnessing community: radically forgiven, radically forgiving. We are to forgive the inexcusable with extravagance, freely and without wanting revenge or justification. This does not mean that we forget the deep pain that others may have caused us, especially in the case of those who have been abused. We may need to establish healthy boundaries, depending on the circumstances. Yet we can extend forgiveness because *Our Father in heaven*, holy and merciful, has forgiven us. We take his name. We take his character. We hear his teaching. We see the model of his Son on the cross. We know that it is possible, because we also see those who are only human, such as Stephen, live it out in the hardest of circumstances.

So, we too forgive, even when we do not want to. Even when it is the hardest thing we must do. We forgive. We forgive. We forgive. For when we do, we see *God's kingdom come, his will be done, on earth as it is in heaven*. We see a gospel community emerge.

Formation questions

1 Identify ways in which you have experienced forgiveness from God and from others.

2 In what ways are you aware of the forgiveness process, and are you able to distinguish forgiving from excusing or glossing over injuries?

3 Stephen prayed, 'Lord, don't charge them with this sin!' What are you 'charging' someone with or holding against another person? Against God? Where has unforgiveness set in?

4 What 'inexcusable' thing, as C. S. Lewis defines it, do you need to forgive in another, knowing that the inexcusable has been forgiven in you?

5 Considering the radical, supernatural nature of forgiveness, how can you demonstrate that personally?

6 In what ways does your outward-focused Jesus community encourage and promote giving, experiencing and knowing forgiveness? How can you further nurture this posture within the church or community of which you are a part?

18

Formed to . . . regenerate

The joy of re-creation

Within missional contexts, we often talk about the weariness that comes with accumulated years of giving out. Sometimes it is referred to as 'burnout', where the tank is not just depleted but has run dry, and nothing seems to refill it. We often concentrate on what not to do, skirting around the edges of the idea of *Sabbath rhythm* – a way of life we are invited into as God's people. This Sabbath space of rest and play, re-creation and regeneration, is a wondrous place for deeper formation, helping to strengthen our inner being as we continue to partner with Christ in the world.

The practice of Sabbath began at creation and stretches throughout the landscape of Scripture. It is about rest, yes, but it is also about much more than ceasing to *do*. It is about trusting who God is and who we are in him. As A. W. Tozer writes:

> the presence of God is the central fact of Christianity . . . Our part is to yield and trust . . . It is not something we do, it is what comes to us when we cease to do. His own meekness, that is the rest.[1]

It is what comes to us when we cease to do. That is powerful! When we cease to do, when we release control, we may finally realise how much busyness crowds our life, how firmly we are holding on to certain things, and what the noise drowns out. As Rich Villodas comments: 'Our world continues on faster and busier, and we are reminded that our souls were not created for the kind of speed to which we have grown accustomed.'[2] When we cease to do, we may become aware of how much we need the 'doing' rather than the 'doing' needing us. When we cease to do, it might become clear just how much of our identity is tied to how productive we are. Without living in rhythm with the One, we may be active, but our busyness will lack 'acute spiritual perception'[3] and will soon turn into white noise, Christian busyness.

Perhaps the temptation towards a busy lifestyle is greater in time-orientated cultures such as Australia, or those cultures that value productivity and efficiency. It is not at all uncommon for Aussies to fill every moment with noise and movement. In a culture where busyness is valued, granting an intangible status, where productivity and efficiency show worth, it is counterintuitive to stop. In a society where noise and distractions are constantly besieging us via technology and media, where the world's mesmerising speed has, more often than not, 'caused our connections with God and others to be incredibly superficial',[4] it is countercultural to step away from the distractions and listen to the Lord. Cultivating spiritual reflection and attuning ourselves to God's voice above others is difficult and takes discipline. Without intentionally fostering this posture, the wheels will just keep spinning. Without yielding such busyness and distractions to the Lord, when we finally look up, the hours or years will have passed us by.

Add to this the tendency towards self-reliance, where God's people inadvertently attempt to contain him. Charles Kraft explains further:

Since we believe our achievements have come through unaided human effort, we focus on human accomplishments and abilities . . . Though human accomplishment is indeed impressive, many seem to believe that there are no limits to it; and, of course, no outside spiritual assistance is needed.[5]

These abilities that Kraft mentions above are both a gift from God and a temptation. With such a strong cultural influence, self-reliance has become the default position for many of those with cultural or personality leanings towards this lure. 'Lead us not into temptation,' Jesus taught us to pray. This temptation, as David Garland helpfully pinpoints, is for God's people to exalt their own names rather than God's, to do their own will rather than God's, to establish their own kingdom rather than God's. It is a very real, although often subtle and unacknowledged, temptation. We can exalt our own names by establishing our own reputations and ensuring our own legacy. We can do our own will, motivated by our own gifts or capacity or insecurities or unredeemed internal drive, our dark side. We can establish our own kingdom through our business or church, our missional community or sphere of influence. However, keeping Sabbath

is a publicly enacted sign of our trust that God keeps the world, therefore we do not have to. God welcomes our labours, but our contributions to the world have their limits. If even God trusted creation enough to be confident that the world would continue while God rested, so should we.[6]

We have a choice. Will we lead the way or let God lead? Will we merely do, or do out of first being? Will we, no matter what the cost, even if it means 'ceasing', nurture a lifelong habit of spiritual responsiveness? Will we yield complete control to the Spirit, who is given by the Father and represents the Son? This choice often appears through confronting challenges. Our sinful nature is spotlighted, and our motivations are exposed, especially if we are allowing the Spirit consistent access to our lives. For as 'we connect with the Spirit through yielding and submission, we are more open to God, more sensitive to God's presence, more discerning of God's will, more humble in the pattern of Jesus'.[7]

But how does this relate to Jesus-centred, outward-focused communities?

As Henri Nouwen echoed Mother Teresa: 'Ministry can be fruitful only if it grows out of a direct and intimate encounter with our Lord.'[8] As we see in Scripture, Jesus modelled this for us. It comes up time and again throughout John's Gospel. Jesus found time and space to meet with the Father, to hear from him and minister out of that place of communion. This practice was integral to his life and work. He acted out of obedience to the Father (John 15:10). His words belonged to the Father who sent him (John 14:24b).

When we live in step with the One, attentively listening to his voice, centring ourselves on him above all else, we guard against losing heart amid the needs and demands of missional living. Then, as Brennan Manning writes, we are 'redefining and reaffirming our identity with Jesus, measuring ourselves against him',[9] and not against our success as gospel people.

A Sabbath lifestyle – a lifestyle of ceasing and yielding with a regular rhythm – reminds us that our first calling is to walk in tempo with our Lord. The minute we feel ourselves getting out of kilter, we pause, recalibrate, and pay attention *again* to the whisper of the Spirit. We listen to Jesus, our Christ, for all things are from him and through him and to him (Romans 11:36). We undergo 'the great reversal: from being the subject who controls all other things to being a person who is shaped by the presence, purpose and power of God in all things'.[10] And we invite the Spirit of God to pervade and invade us as we release control to him again.

I am relearning the practice of life-giving regeneration and re-creation. For a time, I stumbled into the somewhat comic misconception that when I had to rest, I had to cease from doing, completely. Not ceasing as a posture, as we have just explored, or ceasing control of things, but literally becoming a lazy person, lying prostrate! Because recreational options were limited in the city where I lived, I would stick on a film and disconnect. It was easy and fun, but I found at the end of it that I did not always feel rested.

Through some reading on silence, I began to consider what was life-giving for me. I started to wrestle with the difference between just rest and life-giving rest or re-creation, regeneration. Others have learned this lesson well. Eugene Peterson recalls: 'On Sabbath we would do nothing that was necessary, obligatory, "useful." We would set the day apart for the unfettered, the free, the unearned. Pray and play.'[11] I have witnessed a family regenerate by sticking on loud music and having a dance party in the living room. For others, it is a games night or coffee with a friend. For others still, it is silence and solitude, reading a book, or going for a walk in the lush greenery of nature, a long run, or engaging in artistic expression. What works for one may not work for the next person. For me, it often includes a rambling walk with my camera. That is life-giving, regenerative, bringing with it a form of re-creation.

We began this book by exploring the role of the Spirit in formation: the formation of creation; the formation of the tabernacle and the enabling of artisans; the formation of Jesus' life and ministry on earth, the early church, and the people of God into those who look more and more like Christ. As we continue intentionally to nurture our formation into Jesus-centred, outward-focused gospel people through the Spirit's eternal movement, we invite him, too, into the activity of re-creation. We ask him and prioritise space for him to continue regenerating us for his purposes, filling us up as we spill out for the sake of others.

Formation questions

1 What is your biblical understanding of Sabbath, this gift to us from God (Exodus 16:29; Mark 2:23–8)?

2 Are you living in a Sabbath rhythm? If so, what does that look like?

3 If you are not exercising a Sabbath rhythm, what is this communicating to those you are discipling or to your family? What are you indirectly telling God?

4 What do you need to cease from and yield to the Lord?

5 What is life-giving for you?

6 How is your practice (or lack thereof) of Sabbath witnessing to those around you?

Final thoughts

When I first wrote these words, my sabbatical was almost over. I had only one full week left. I was still down by the water, walking along the coast each day during the two hours when we were allowed outside for exercise. On that day of writing, the sun was shining, but I woke with the weariness that can come from weeks of Covid lockdown, especially when it is done away from home. I was missing my various communities.

I had reached for my phone that morning, exchanging a couple of messages with a sister-friend. Then I saw another work-related discussion. I read it through. I was tempted to jump in, engage, and add my two cents' worth of insight. No. I was on sabbatical, at least for a little longer. *Just say no.* Oh, I was tempted, perhaps if for no other reason than to break the Groundhog Day monotony of lockdown.

But then, I read these words in a book by Henri Nouwen:

Solitude is the furnace of transformation . . . it is a place of conversion, the place where the old self dies and the new self is born, the place where the emergence of the new man and the new woman occurs.[1]

And in the next chapter: 'Many experience silence not as full and rich, but as empty and hollow.'[2]

This could have been about the deep lessons of solitude, but it wasn't. It could have been about ceasing work and practising Sabbath, but it wasn't. It could have been about identity, but it wasn't. In that moment, it was about responding to whatever God was using to turn me more fully to himself. It was about being alive to the Spirit's shaping work, his whisper and invitation. Right then, I asked the Lord to change my heart, to enable a holy exchange – the empty and hollow traded for the full and rich. And graciously, it was as if he took me by the shoulders and turned me around. Over the hours that followed, the edginess vanished, transforming the remaining sabbatical days. The Spirit continued directing the ebb and flow of high tide and low tide, filling up and spilling out, wonder and worship.

Paying attention to the Spirit's activity, this time as he formed *from* the material of a longer-than-expected Covid isolation, was a gift. It was sacred space, full and rich, set apart for the profound converting touch of the Spirit. He was not, is not, finished yet. Even with only a handful of days left of that set-aside season before I returned to the normal engagement of my role, he was committed to his work of strengthening my inner being, of forming me for his mission in the world, of shaping me for the sake of others. He was committed then. He is committed now. His re-creating breath will continue until this moment becomes our always-future with him.

May it be so with you, too, as you fling yourself wide open in invitation to the God of all things, made alive through the Spirit's faithful and creative work within us. God loves to form us into the likeness of Christ for the sake of this world of his.

As I wrote in the early pages of this book, may we all continue to be a people filled up *by* him and spilling out *for* him, in whatever shape or form that may take, whatever the circumstances may be. May we realise with greater certainty and joy that we have been formed for God's mission to be Christ-honouring, outward-focused people.

In this life, may your formation into Christ-form never end, and may you never want it to.

And through this cyclical motion of formation, may others see, desire and come to know God revealed in Christ, our hope, joy and purpose.

Until that day . . .

. . . when formation for God's mission in the world is no longer needed.

Saying thanks

Thank you, precious Father, for sending your Son to save us and the Spirit of your Son to shape us. I'm so grateful for the leadership of the Spirit as I prayed and walked and wrote, and that, through prayer, he led me right up to the door of SPCK.

Thank you, Elizabeth Neep, for being open to a random stranger reaching out via the SPCK submissions page. I still find it miraculous that you said yes – yes to reading my manuscript and that you saw something in it, yes to continuing in conversation, yes to meeting for coffee when I was over in the UK for work, and finally that you said yes on behalf of SPCK to put these words into print. To paraphrase Marilynne Robinson, you have been God's good gift to me, welcoming me into the world of publishing with open arms and a dimpled smile.

I am grateful to all those at SPCK London who have journeyed with me: Katherine Venn, Philip Law and Lauren Windle, as you helped me transform from a writer to an author. To Dan, who created such a beautiful and moving book cover. To Joy and Mollie for their sharp eyes and hospitable professionalism. And to the many others who partnered with me in this endeavour. Thank you for your faithful and hard work.

Covid-19 helped me fall in love with my church community in deeper ways, and I continue to give thanks for this multicultural group of hungry followers of Jesus. Thank you for your spiritual leadership, Pastor Tan and XuPing, and my local church in Melbourne, for doing life together with me, for inviting me to speak regularly into your lives through teaching, for your support and prayers and joy. I love that we belong to one another.

My heart fills with gratitude for those of you who travelled this strange and vulnerable journey with me in significant ways. Thank you for your belief and encouragement. My Regional Leadership Team, for releasing me into this sabbatical time and believing that I had something to offer through writing; Auntie Maus and Uncle John, for quickly inviting me to house-sit during my sabbatical (it was the perfect provision, especially as we went into our second long lockdown in Melbourne); Jo, for praying with and for me, and broadening my understanding of who the audience could be; Ash and Sue, for being heart friends with whom I felt safe enough to share the very first draft of this book; Salote, for being my cousin/sister, who held me firm when I wavered, and cheered me on when I needed it; the Laughing Ladies, for your long and unconditional love; each of you whose stories are tucked away in the pages of this book (some of whose names have been changed), adding colour and texture to this offering; those of you who, over the years, have been fellow travellers with me on various writing platforms. And Mum and Dad, my truest and most consistent disciplers, mentors and encouragers. I am so grateful to the Lord for giving you to me.

Thank you all for being my people on this sacred book journey.

Notes

A word before

1 Richard J. Foster, *Celebration of Discipline: The path to spiritual growth* (San Francisco, CA: Harper & Row, 1988), p. 175.
2 'The LORD replied, "I will personally go with you, Moses, and I will give you rest . . ."' (Exodus 33:14).

Unformed

1 Erwin Raphael McManus, *The Artisan Soul: Crafting your life into a work of art* (New York, NY: HarperCollins, 2014), p. 31.
2 Rich Villodas, *The Deeply Formed Life: Five transformative values to root us in the way of Jesus* (Colorado Springs, CO: WaterBrook, 2020), p. 152.

1 Formed by . . .

1 Unless otherwise specified, all Scripture citations are taken from the New Living Translation (NLT).
2 Sara Lubbers, *Always Love: The timeless story of God's heart for the world and what it means for you* (Llantwit Major: Peregrini Press, 2019), p. 1.
3 Pronounced 'ruach' with the final consonant sounding like 'ch' in Scottish 'loch'.
4 'My dear children, for whom I am again in the pains of childbirth until Christ is formed in you' (Galatians 4:19 NIV).
5 Harold W. Hoehner, *Ephesians: An exegetical commentary* (Grand Rapids, MI: Baker Academic, 2002), p. 705.

2 Formed through . . .

1 Siang-Yang Tan and Douglas H. Gregg, *Disciplines of the Holy Spirit: How to connect to the Spirit's power and presence* (Grand Rapids, MI: Zondervan, 1997), p. 66.

2 Edward M. Bounds, *E. M. Bounds on Prayer* (New Kensington, PA: Whitaker House, 1997), p. 154.

3 H. E. Fosdick, *The Meaning of Prayer* (London: SCM Press, 1954), p. 60.

4 James G. S. S. Thomson, *The Praying Christ: A study of Jesus' doctrine and practice of prayer* (Grand Rapids, MI: Eerdmans, 1959), p. 43.

5 Kathryn R. Pocklington, 'The Role of Prayer in Mission Formation: From Africa to Australia', doctoral dissertation, Fuller Theological Seminary, School of Intercultural Studies, 2017: https://www. proquest.com/docview/1968594326/61FB1656B134472PQ/1 (accessed 11 July 2021).

6 Pocklington, 'The Role of Prayer'.

7 Pocklington, 'The Role of Prayer'.

8 Pocklington, 'The Role of Prayer'.

9 Pocklington, 'The Role of Prayer'.

10 N. T. Wright, *The Lord and His Prayer* (Grand Rapids, MI: Eerdmans and Forward Movement Publications, 1997), pp. 18–19.

11 Walter C. Wright, *Relational Leadership: A biblical model for influence and service* (Carlisle: Paternoster, 2000), p. 187.

3 Formed for . . .

1 The website of the Catholic Mission, Australia, has since been edited. Please note alternative citing in Kathryn R. Pocklington, 'The Role of Prayer in Mission Formation: From Africa to Australia', doctoral dissertation, Fuller Theological Seminary, School of Intercultural Studies, 2017, p. 146.

2 The website of the Catholic Social Services Victoria has since been edited. Please note alternative citing in Pocklington, 'The Role of Prayer', p. 146.

3 M. Robert Mulholland Jr and Ruth Haley Barton, *Invitation to a Journey: A road map for spiritual formation*, rev. edn (Downers Grove, IL: InterVarsity Press, 2016).

4 Eugene H. Peterson, *The Message Remix: The Bible in contemporary language* (Colorado Springs, CO: NavPress, 2006), p. 1795.

5 Eugene H. Peterson, *On Living Well: Brief reflections on wisdom for*

walking in the way of Jesus (Colorado Springs, CO: WaterBrook, 2021), Kindle location 26.

4 Formed from . . . family

1 Robert Atkinson, *The Life Story Interview* (Thousand Oaks, CA: SAGE, 1998), pp. 73, 20.

2 Irving Seidman, *Interviewing as Qualitative Research: A guide for researchers in education and the social sciences*, 4th edn (New York, NY: Teachers College Press, 2013), Kindle location 291.

3 Eugene H. Peterson, *The Pastor: A memoir* (New York, NY: HarperCollins, 2011), p. 40.

4 Ruth Haley Barton, *Invitation to Solitude and Silence: Experiencing God's transforming presence* (Downers Grove, IL: InterVarsity Press, 2010), Kindle location 78.

5 M. Robert Mulholland Jr and Ruth Haley Barton, *Invitation to a Journey: A road map for spiritual formation*, rev. edn (Downers Grove, IL: InterVarsity Press, 2016), p. 16.

5 Formed from . . . influence

1 Gordon MacDonald, *A Resilient Life: You can move ahead no matter what* (Nashville, TN: Thomas Nelson, 2009), p. 111. The other two categories are: major ideas that have guided us, whether honourable or corrupt; and life-changing critical events, whether happy or sad.

2 Ruth Wall, 'Teaching and Learning to Nurture Spirituality', in John Amalraj, Geoffrey W. Hahn and William David Taylor (eds), *Spirituality in Mission: Embracing the lifelong journey*, Globalization of Mission Series (Pasadena, CA: William Carey Library, 2018), Kindle location 5525.

3 Gary L. McIntosh and Samuel D. Rima Sr, *Overcoming the Dark Side of Leadership: How to become an effective leader by confronting potential failures* (Grand Rapids, MI: Baker, 2007), Kindle location 1863.

4 McIntosh and Rima, *Overcoming the Dark Side*, Kindle location 2044.

6 Formed from . . . pain

1 Frederick Buechner, *The Clown in the Belfry: Writings on faith and fiction* (San Francisco, CA: HarperCollins, 1992), p. 99.

2 Ajith Fernando, *The Call to Joy and Pain: Embracing suffering in your ministry* (Wheaton, IL: Crossway, 2007), Kindle locations 556, 561.

3 Larry Crabb, *Shattered Dreams: God's unexpected path to joy* (Colorado Springs, CO: WaterBrook, 2012), p. 4.

4 'We can rejoice, too, when we run into problems and trials, for we know that they help us develop endurance. And endurance develops strength of character, and character strengthens our confident hope of salvation. And this hope will not lead to disappointment. For we know how dearly God loves us, because he has given us the Holy Spirit to fill our hearts with his love' (Romans 5:3–5).

5 Fernando, *The Call to Joy and Pain*, p. 102.

6 Tiffany Clark, 'The Road from Broken', messytheology, 18 February 2015: https://messytheology.wordpress.com/category/suffering-2 (accessed 23 November 2021).

7 Formed from . . . gift-mix

1 This quote and the one following were found on Kaye Redman's previous website and are used by permission of the artist. Please go to www.kayeredman.com for more of Kaye's current story.

2 Erwin Raphael McManus, *The Artisan Soul: Crafting your life into a work of art* (New York, NY: HarperCollins, 2014), pp. 61–2.

3 Those described in Romans 12:6–8; 1 Corinthians 12:8–10; Ephesians 4:11; and 1 Peter 4:(9)10–11.

4 'To one person the Spirit gives the ability to give wise advice; to another the same Spirit gives a message of special knowledge' (1 Corinthians 12:8).

5 Ken Gire, *Windows of the Soul: Experiencing God in new ways* (Grand Rapids, MI: Zondervan, 1996), p. 11.

6 Marilynne Robinson, *Gilead* (Vision Australia Information and Library Service, 2004), p. 60.

7 Christine D. Pohl, *Living into Community: Cultivating practices that sustain us* (Grand Rapids, MI: Eerdmans, 2012), p. 75.

8 Formed from . . . learning

1 Erin Meyer, *The Culture Map: Decoding how people think, lead, and get things done across cultures* (New York, NY: Public Affairs, 2015).

2 Siang-Yang Tan and Douglas H. Gregg, *Disciplines of the Holy Spirit: How to connect to the Spirit's power and presence* (Grand Rapids, MI: Zondervan, 1997), p. 50.

3 Siang-Yang Tan, *Full Service: Moving from self-serve Christianity to total servanthood* (Ada, MI: Baker, 2006), Kindle location 1632.

4 Ed Scheuerman, *Knowing God to Make Him Known: Living out the attributes of God cross-culturally* (Eugene, OR: Wipf & Stock, 2021), p. 61.

5 Brené Brown, *Dare to Lead: Brave work. Tough conversations. Whole hearts* (New York, NY: Random House, 2018), p. 73.

6 Doug Sherman and William Hendricks, *Your Work Matters to God* (Colorado Springs, CO: NavPress, 1987), p. 167.

9 Formed from . . . culture

1 Ruth Van Reken, 'Who Are Cross Cultural Kids?', Cross Cultural Kids (blog): www.crossculturalkid.org/who-are-cross-cultural-kids (accessed 29 October 2021).

2 This is a direct quote from a video made of the interview within the 'Leading in Complexity' session, held in March 2019.

3 Timothy C. Tennent, *Invitation to World Missions: A Trinitarian missiology for the twenty-first century* (Grand Rapids, MI: Kregel Academic, 2010), p. 51.

4 Adrian Pei, *The Minority Experience: Navigating emotional and organizational realities* (Downers Grove, IL: InterVarsity Press, 2018), p. 38.

5 Mitch Kim, 'Black Lives Matter – A Sign', Wellspring Alliance Church (blog): https://wellspringalliance.net/2020/10/08/black-lives-matter-a-sign (accessed 18 September 2021).

6 Pei, *The Minority Experience*, p. 25.

7 Tracey Michae'l Lewis-Giggetts, 'Love Lifted Me: Subverting shame narratives and legitimizing vulnerability as a mechanism for healing women in the black church', in Tarana Burke and Brené Brown (eds),

You Are Your Best Thing: Vulnerability, shame resilience, and the black experience – an anthology (New York, NY; Random House, 2021), p. 57.

8 Lewis-Giggetts, 'Love Lifted Me', p. 64.

9 Solomon Aryeetey, '"Sebi Tafratse" (With All Due Respects): A word to the West from "the rest"', *Evangelical MIssions Quarterly* 49, no. 2 (2013): p. 173: https://missionexus.org/sebi-tafratse-with-all-due-respects-a-word-to-the-west-from-the-rest (accessed 22 July 2021).

10 Formed from . . . age

1 K. John Amalraj, 'What Shapes Our Spirituality in Missions?', in John Amalraj, Geoffrey W. Hahn and William David Taylor (eds), *Spirituality in Mission: Embracing the lifelong journey*, Globalization of Mission Series (Pasadena, CA: William Carey Library, 2018).

2 Amalraj, 'What Shapes Our Spirituality in Missions?', Kindle location 982.

11 Formed from . . . gender: women

1 Dominique DuBois Gilliard, *Subversive Witness: Scripture's call to leverage privilege* (Grand Rapids, MI: Zondervan, 2021), p. xiii.

2 Gilliard, *Subversive Witness*, p. 17.

3 Gilliard, *Subversive Witness*, p. 17.

4 Mary T. Lederleitner, *Women in God's Mission: Accepting the invitation to serve and lead* (Downers Grove, IL: InterVarsity Press, 2018), Kindle location 704.

5 Jack Zenger, 'The Confidence Gap in Men and Women: Why it matters and how to overcome it', Forbes, 5 April 2018: https://www.forbes.com/sites/jackzenger/2018/04/08/the-confidence-gap-in-men-and-women-why-it-matters-and-how-to-overcome-it (accessed 23 July 2021).

6 Nancy F. Clark, 'Act Now to Shrink the Confidence Gap', WomensMedia, Forbes, 28 April 2014: https://www.forbes.com/sites/womensmedia/2014/04/28/act-now-to-shrink-the-confidence-gap (accessed 11 August 2021).

12 Formed from . . . gender: men

1 Mary T. Lederleitner, *Women in God's Mission: Accepting the invitation to serve and lead* (Downers Grove, IL: InterVarsity Press, 2018), Kindle location 2131.

2 Lederleitner, *Women in God's Mission*, Kindle location 2138.

3 Sue Edwards, Kelley Mathews and Henry J. Rogers, *Mixed Ministry: Working together as brothers and sisters in an oversexed society* (Grand Rapids, MI: Kregel Academic, 2008), pp. 126–7.

4 Isabel Allende, *The Soul of a Woman* (London: Bloomsbury Circus, 2020), p. 34.

13 Formed from . . . team

1 M. Robert Mulholland Jr and Ruth Haley Barton, *Invitation to a Journey: A road map for spiritual formation*, rev. edn (Downers Grove, IL: InterVarsity Press, 2016), p. 51.

2 Eugene H. Peterson, *The Pastor: A memoir* (New York, NY: HarperCollins, 2011), p. 158.

3 Christine D. Pohl, *Living into Community: Cultivating practices that sustain us* (Grand Rapids, MI: Eerdmans, 2012), p. 6.

4 Pohl, *Living into Community*, p. 7.

5 Eugene H. Peterson, *As Kingfishers Catch Fire: A conversation on the ways of God formed by the words of God* (Colorado Springs, CO: WaterBrook, 2017), p. 311.

14 Formed from . . . those we serve

1 Ajith Fernando, *The Call to Joy and Pain: Embracing suffering in your ministry* (Wheaton, IL: Crossway, 2007), p. 132.

2 Kelly Malone, *Hearing Christ's Voice: Living and proclaiming the gospel in an embattled world* (Garland, TX: Hannibal Books, 2006), Kindle location 148.

3 Elliot D. Stephens, 'Retention and Onboarding: Are we ready to ask the hard questions?', *Evangelical Missions Quarterly* 55, no. 4 (2019): 17: https://missionexus.org/retention-and-onboarding-are-we-ready-to-ask-the-hard-questions (accessed 6 December 2021).

4 Commission on World Mission and Evangelism, 'Together towards

Life: Mission and evangelism in changing landscapes', World
Council of Churches, 6 September 2012, Affirmation 71: https://www.
oikoumene.org/resources/documents/together-towards-life-mission-
and-evangelism-in-changing-landscapes (accessed 24 July 2021).

15 Formed to . . . trust

1 Tony Horsfall and Debbie Hawker, *Resilience in Life and Faith:
  Finding your strength in God* (Abingdon: Bible Reading Fellowship,
  2019), p. 145.

2 Siang-Yang Tan and Douglas H. Gregg, *Disciplines of the Holy Spirit:
  How to connect to the Spirit's power and presence* (Grand Rapids, MI:
  Zondervan, 1997), pp. 47, 48.

3 Ken Gire, *Windows of the Soul: Experiencing God in new ways* (Grand
  Rapids, MI: Zondervan, 1996), p. 148.

4 Rob Reimer, *Soul Care: Seven transformational principles for a
  healthy soul* (Franklin, TN: Carpenter's Son Publishing, 2016),
  p. 225.

5 Eugene H. Peterson, *The Pastor: A memoir* (New York, NY:
  HarperCollins, 2011), p. 217.

6 '. . . Christ Jesus, who gives us hope' (1 Timothy 1:1).

7 'Faith shows the reality of what we hope for . . .' (Hebrews 11:1).

8 See 1 Timothy 6:17; Titus 1:2; 2:13; Hebrews 6:19; 1 Peter 1:21, to list
  just a small selection of passages regarding hope.

9 Brené Brown, *The Gifts of Imperfection: Let go of who you think you're
  supposed to be and embrace who you are* (Center City, MO: Hazelden,
  2010), Kindle locations 1174–8.

16 Formed to . . . be open

1 Geert Hofstede was a Dutch social scientist who pioneered
  comparative intercultural research. Through the extensive data
  collected through his years with IMB International, six 'dimensions'
  of culture emerged which have established a current framework for
  cultural comparison.

2 Robert K. Greenleaf et al., *The Servant-Leader Within: A
  transformative path* (Mahwah, NJ: Paulist Press, 2003), p. 103.

3 William P. Young, *The Shack* (Newbury Park, CA: Windblown Media, 2007), p. 205.

4 Young, *The Shack*, p. 205.

5 Ronald A. Heifetz and M. Linsky, *Leadership on the Line: Staying alive through the dangers of leading* (Boston, MA: Harvard Business School Press, 2002), p. 227.

6 Heifetz and Linsky, *Leadership on the Line*, pp. 229–30.

7 Daniel Goleman, *Social Intelligence: The new science of human relationships* (New York, NY: Bantam, 2006), Kindle locations 3185–7.

17 Formed to . . . forgive

1 N. T. Wright, *The Lord and His Prayer* (Grand Rapids, MI: Eerdmans and Forward Movement Publications, 1997), p. 54.

2 H. French, 'The Lord's Prayer: A primer on mission in the way of Jesus', *Word & World* 22, no. 1 (2002): p. 25.

3 Eugene H. Peterson, 'Prayers of Jesus: The Johannine legacy', in *Regent College Lectures – Jesus & Prayer* (Vancouver: Regent College, 1997), 55:16.

4 French, 'The Lord's Prayer', p. 25.

5 See the website Peacewise: building peacemakers for life for more on conflict resolution and processes of forgiveness.

6 Joel B. Green, 'Jesus on the Mount of Olives (Luke 22:39–46): Tradition and theology', *Journal for the Study of the New Testament* 26 (1986): p. 39.

18 Formed to . . . regenerate

1 A. W. Tozer, *The Pursuit of God*, ed. Ruth Zetek (Abbotsford, WI: Aneko Press, 2015), pp. 19, 23, 49.

2 Rich Villodas, *The Deeply Formed Life: Five transformative values to root us in the way of Jesus* (Colorado Springs, CO: WaterBrook, 2020), p. 24.

3 Tozer, *The Pursuit of God*, p. 28.

4 Villodas, *The Deeply Formed Life*, p. 27.

5 Charles H. Kraft, *Christianity with Power: Your worldview and your*

experience of the supernatural (Ann Arbor, MI: Vine Books, 1989), p. 30.

6 William Willimon, *Pastor: The theology and practice of ordained ministry* (Nashville, TN: Abingdon Press, 2000), p. 329.

7 Siang-Yang Tan and Douglas H. Gregg, *Disciplines of the Holy Spirit: How to connect to the Spirit's power and presence* (Grand Rapids, MI: Zondervan, 1997), p. 114.

8 Henri J. M. Nouwen, *The Way of the Heart: The spirituality of the desert fathers and mothers* (New York, NY: HarperCollins, 2016), p. 14.

9 Brennan Manning, *The Signature of Jesus* (Sisters, OR: Multnomah Books, 1996), p. 90.

10 M. Robert Mulholland Jr and Ruth Haley Barton, *Invitation to a Journey: A road map for spiritual formation*, rev. edn (Downers Grove, IL: InterVarsity Press, 2016), p. 33.

11 Eugene H. Peterson, *The Pastor: A memoir* (New York, NY: HarperCollins, 2011), p. 311.

Final thoughts

1 Henri J. M. Nouwen, *The Way of the Heart: The spirituality of the desert fathers and mothers* (New York, NY: HarperCollins, 2016), pp. 10, 11.

2 Nouwen, *The Way of the Heart*, p. 29.

Bibliography

Allende, Isabel. *The Soul of a Woman* (London: Bloomsbury Circus, 2020).

Amalraj, K. John. 'What Shapes Our Spirituality in Missions?', in John Amalraj, Geoffrey W. Hahn and William David Taylor (eds), *Spirituality in Mission: Embracing the lifelong journey*, Globalization of Mission Series (Pasadena, CA: William Carey Library, 2018).

Aryeetey, Solomon. '"Sebi Tafratse" (With All Due Respects): A word to the West from "the rest"', *Evangelical MIssions Quarterly* 49, no. 2 (2013): pp. 166–74: https://missionexus.org/sebi-tafratse-with-all-due-respects-a-word-to-the-west-from-the-rest (accessed 22 September 2021).

Atkinson, Robert. *The Life Story Interview* (Thousand Oaks, CA: SAGE, 1998).

Barton, Ruth Haley. *Invitation to Solitude and Silence: Experiencing God's transforming presence* (Downers Grove, IL: InterVarsity Press, 2010).

Bounds, Edward M. *E. M. Bounds on Prayer* (New Kensington, PA: Whitaker House, 1997).

Brown, Brené. *Dare to Lead: Brave work. Tough conversations. Whole hearts* (New York, NY: Random House, 2018.

——. *The Gifts of Imperfection: Let go of who you think you're supposed to be and embrace who you are* (Center City, MO: Hazelden, 2010).

Buechner, Frederick. *The Clown in the Belfry: Writings on faith and fiction* (San Francisco, CA: HarperCollins, 1992).

Clark, Nancy F. 'Act Now to Shrink the Confidence Gap', WomensMedia, Forbes, 28 April 2014: https://www.forbes.com/sites/womensmedia/2014/04/28/act-now-to-shrink-the-confidence-gap (accessed 11 August 2021).

Clark, Tiffany. 'The Road from Broken', messytheology, 18 February 2015: https://messytheology.wordpress.com/category/suffering-2 (accessed 23 November 2021).

Commission on World Mission and Evangelism. 'Together towards Life:

Mission and evangelism in changing landscapes', World Council of
   Churches, 6 September 2012: https://www.oikoumene.org/resources/
   documents/together-towards-life-mission-and-evangelism-in-
   changing-landscapes (accessed 24 July 2021).
Crabb, Larry. *Shattered Dreams: God's unexpected path to joy* (Colorado
   Springs, CO: WaterBrook, 2012).
Edwards, Sue, Kelley Mathews and Henry J. Rogers. *Mixed Ministry:
   Working together as brothers and sisters in an oversexed society* (Grand
   Rapids, MI: Kregel Academic, 2008).
Fernando, Ajith. *The Call to Joy and Pain: Embracing suffering in your
   ministry* (Wheaton, IL: Crossway, 2007).
Fosdick, H. E. *The Meaning of Prayer* (London: SCM Press, 1954).
Foster, Richard J. *Celebration of Discipline: The path to spiritual growth*
   (San Francisco, CA: Harper & Row, 1988).
French, H. 'The Lord's Prayer: A primer on mission in the way of Jesus',
   Word & World 22, no. 1 (2002): pp. 18–26.
Gilliard, Dominique DuBois. *Subversive Witness: Scripture's call to
   leverage privilege* (Grand Rapids, MI: Zondervan, 2021).
Gire, Ken. *Windows of the Soul: Experiencing God in new ways* (Grand
   Rapids, MI: Zondervan, 1996).
Goleman, Daniel. *Social Intelligence: The new science of human
   relationships* (New York, NY: Bantam, 2006).
Green, Joel B. 'Jesus on the Mount of Olives (Luke 22:39–46): Tradition
   and theology', *Journal for the Study of the New Testament* 26 (1986):
   pp. 29–48.
Greenleaf, Robert K., Hamilton Beazley, Julie Beggs and Larry C. Spears.
   The Servant-Leader Within: A transformative path (Mahwah, NJ:
   Paulist Press, 2003).
Heifetz, Ronald A. and M. Linsky. *Leadership on the Line: Staying alive
   through the dangers of leading* (Boston, MA: Harvard Business School
   Press, 2002).
Hoehner, Harold W. *Ephesians: An exegetical commentary* (Grand
   Rapids, MI: Baker Academic, 2002).
Horsfall, Tony and Debbie Hawker. *Resilience in Life and Faith: Finding
   your strength in God* (Abingdon: Bible Reading Fellowship, 2019).

Kim, Mitch. 'Black Lives Matter – A Sign', Wellspring Alliance Church (blog): https://wellspringalliance.net/2020/10/08/black-lives-matter-a-sign (accessed 18 September 2021).

Kraft, Charles H. *Christianity with Power: Your worldview and your experience of the supernatural* (Ann Arbor, MI: Vine Books, 1989).

Lederleitner, Mary T. *Women in God's Mission: Accepting the invitation to serve and lead* (Downers Grove, IL: InterVarsity Press, 2018).

Lewis, C. S. *The Weight of Glory* (London: HarperCollins, 2013).

Lewis-Giggetts, Tracey Michae'l. 'Love Lifted Me: Subverting shame narratives and legitimizing vulnerability as a mechanism for healing women in the black church', in Tarana Burke and Brené Brown (eds), *You Are Your Best Thing: Vulnerability, shame resilience, and the black experience – an anthology* (New York, NY: Random House, 2021).

Lubbers, Sara. *Always Love: The timeless story of God's heart for the world and what it means for you* (Llantwit Major: Peregrini Press, 2019).

MacDonald, Gordon. *A Resilient Life: You can move ahead no matter what* (Nashville, TN: Thomas Nelson, 2009).

McIntosh, Gary L., and Samuel D. Rima Sr. *Overcoming the Dark Side of Leadership: How to become an effective leader by confronting potential failures* (Grand Rapids, MI: Baker, 2007).

McManus, Erwin Raphael. *The Artisan Soul: Crafting your life into a work of art* (New York, NY: HarperCollins, 2014).

Malone, Kelly. *Hearing Christ's Voice: Living and proclaiming the gospel in an embattled world* (Garland, TX: Hannibal Books, 2006).

Manning, Brennan. *The Signature of Jesus* (Sisters, OR: Multnomah Books, 1996).

Meyer, Erin. *The Culture Map: Decoding how people think, lead, and get things done across cultures* (New York, NY: Public Affairs, 2015).

Mulholland Jr, M. Robert and Ruth Haley Barton. *Invitation to a Journey: A road map for spiritual formation*, rev. edn (Downers Grove, IL: InterVarsity Press, 2016).

Nouwen, Henri J. M. *The Way of the Heart: The spirituality of the desert fathers and mothers* (New York, NY: HarperCollins, 2016).

Pei, Adrian. *The Minority Experience: Navigating emotional and organizational realities* (Downers Grove, IL: InterVarsity Press, 2018).

Peterson, Eugene H. *As Kingfishers Catch Fire: A conversation on the ways of God formed by the words of God* (Colorado Springs, CO: WaterBrook, 2017).

——. *The Message Remix: The Bible in contemporary language* (Colorado Springs, CO: NavPress, 2006).

——. *On Living Well: Brief reflections on wisdom for walking in the way of Jesus* (Colorado Springs, CO: WaterBrook, 2021).

——. *The Pastor: A memoir* (New York, NY: HarperCollins, 2011).

——. 'Prayers of Jesus: The Johannine legacy', in *Regent College Lectures – Jesus & Prayer* (Vancouver: Regent College, 1997).

Pocklington, Kathryn R. 'The Role of Prayer in Mission Formation: From Africa to Australia', doctoral dissertation, Fuller Theological Seminary, School of Intercultural Studies, 2017: https://www.proquest.com/docview/1968594326/61FB1656B134472PQ/1 (accessed 11 July 2021).

Pohl, Christine D. *Living into Community: Cultivating practices that sustain us* (Grand Rapids, MI: Eerdmans, 2012).

Reimer, Rob. *Soul Care: Seven transformational principles for a healthy soul* (Franklin, TN: Carpenter's Son Publishing, 2016).

Robinson, Marilynne. *Gilead* (Vision Australia Information and Library Service, 2004).

Scheuerman, Ed. *Knowing God to Make Him Known: Living out the attributes of God cross-culturally* (Eugene, OR: Wipf & Stock, 2021).

Seidman, Irving. *Interviewing as Qualitative Research: A guide for researchers in education and the social sciences*, 4th edn (New York, NY: Teachers College Press, 2013).

Sherman, Doug and William Hendricks. *Your Work Matters to God* (Colorado Springs, CO: NavPress, 1987).

Stephens, Elliot D. 'Retention and Onboarding: Are we ready to ask the hard questions?', *Evangelical Missions Quarterly* 55, no. 4 (2019): https://missionexus.org/retention-and-onboarding-are-we-ready-to-ask-the-hard-questions (accessed 6 December 2021).

Tan, Siang-Yang. *Full Service: Moving from self-serve Christianity to total servanthood* (Ada, MI: Baker, 2006).

Tan, Siang-Yang and Douglas H. Gregg. *Disciplines of the Holy Spirit:*

How to connect to the Spirit's power and presence (Grand Rapids, MI: Zondervan, 1997).

Tennent, Timothy C. *Invitation to World Missions: A Trinitarian missiology for the twenty-first century* (Grand Rapids, MI: Kregel Academic, 2010).

Thomson, James G. S. S. *The Praying Christ: A study of Jesus' doctrine and practice of prayer* (Grand Rapids, MI: Eerdmans, 1959).

Tozer, A. W. *The Pursuit of God*, ed. Ruth Zetek (Abbotsford, WI: Aneko Press, 2015).

Van Reken, Ruth. 'Who Are Cross Cultural Kids?', Cross Cultural Kids (blog): http://www.crossculturalkid.org/who-are-cross-cultural-kids (accessed 29 October 2021).

Villodas, Rich. *The Deeply Formed Life: Five transformative values to root us in the way of Jesus* (Colorado Springs, CO: WaterBrook, 2020).

Wall, Ruth. 'Teaching and Learning to Nurture Spirituality', in John Amalraj, Geoffrey W. Hahn and William David Taylor (eds), *Spirituality in Mission: Embracing the lifelong journey*, Globalization of Mission Series (Pasadena, CA: William Carey Library, 2018).

Willimon, William. *Pastor: The theology and practice of ordained ministry* (Nashville, TN: Abingdon Press, 2000).

Wright, N. T. *The Lord and His Prayer* (Grand Rapids, MI: Eerdmans and Forward Movement Publications, 1997).

Wright, Walter C. *Relational Leadership: A biblical model for influence and service* (Carlisle: Paternoster, 2000).

Young, William P. *The Shack* (Newbury Park, CA: Windblown Media, 2007).

Zenger, Jack. 'The Confidence Gap in Men and Women: Why it matters and how to overcome it', Forbes, 5 April 2018: https://www.forbes.com/sites/jackzenger/2018/04/08/the-confidence-gap-in-men-and-women-why-it-matters-and-how-to-overcome-it (accessed 23 July 2021).